Social Media
MARKETING
Be Digitally Visible

John Monyjok Maluth

Copyright © 2024 John Monyjok Maluth

ISBN: 9798324522117

Discipleship Press

Web: www.discipleshippress.wordpress.com
Email: maluthabiel@gmail.com

~~~~

+254 797 624 994
+211 927 145 394

P.O. Box 28448-00100, Nairobi Kenya

All rights reserved. No part of this book may be reproduced, stored in a retrieval system, or transmitted in any or by any means – electronic, mechanical, photocopying, recording, or otherwise-without prior permission in writing from the copyright holder.

CONTENTS

PART ONE: THE POWER OF SOCIAL CONNECTION 1

    CHAPTER ONE: WHY SOCIAL MEDIA MATTERS 1
    STORY THREAD 1
    WHAT I TEACH 4
    MY ACTION STEPS 11
    A CLOSING LESSON BEFORE YOU MOVE TO CHAPTER TWO 16
    CHAPTER TWO: BUILDING YOUR ONLINE COMMUNITY 17
    STORY THREAD 17
    WHAT I TEACH 20
    MY ACTION STEPS 32
    EXTRA TEACHING: HOW I KEEP COMMUNITY FROM BECOMING EXHAUSTING 40
    CLOSING MESSAGE FOR THIS CHAPTER 42
    CHAPTER THREE: UNDERSTANDING YOUR AUDIENCE 43
    STORY THREAD 43
    WHAT I TEACH 45
    MY ACTION STEPS 51
    CLOSING LESSON FOR THIS CHAPTER 54

PART TWO: CRAFTING YOUR SOCIAL MEDIA PRESENCE 56

    CHAPTER FOUR: A COMPELLING BRAND STORY 57
    STORY THREAD 57
    WHAT I TEACH 60
    MY ACTION STEPS 67
    CLOSING LESSON FOR THIS CHAPTER 71
    CHAPTER FIVE: CREATING ENGAGING CONTENT 72
    STORY THREAD 72
    WHAT I TEACH 74
    MY ACTION STEPS 83
    CLOSING LESSON FOR THIS CHAPTER 85
    CHAPTER SIX: THE ART OF STORYTELLING 87
    STORY THREAD 87
    WHAT I TEACH 89
    MY ACTION STEPS 96
    CLOSING LESSON FOR THIS CHAPTER 99

PART THREE: ENGAGING WITH YOUR AUDIENCE 101

    CHAPTER SEVEN: SOCIAL MEDIA MANAGEMENT 102
    STORY THREAD 102
    WHAT I TEACH 104
    MY ACTION STEPS 113

- Closing lesson for this chapter..117
- Build a simple media folder structure for fast posting.....................118
- The core rule 118
- Folder structure...118
- Naming rules 120
- Weekly habit 121
- Chapter Eight: The art of conversation...121
- Story thread 121
- What I teach 123
- My action steps...131
- Closing lesson for this chapter...133
- Chapter Nine: Building brand advocacy..135
- Story thread 135
- What I teach 138
- My action steps...145
- Closing lesson for this chapter...148

PART FOUR: MEASURING SUCCESS AND GROWTH 149
- Chapter Ten: Tracking your results..149
- Story thread 149
- What I teach 152
- My action steps...161
- Closing lesson for this chapter...164
- Chapter Eleven: Adapting and updating 166
- Story thread 166
- What I teach 167
- My action steps...176
- Closing lesson for this chapter...179
- Chapter Twelve: Beyond the basics 180
- Story thread 180
- What I teach 182
- My action steps...191
- Closing lesson for this chapter...194
- Appendices and tools (copy-and-use)...195
- Appendix A: 30-day digital visibility plan 195
- The goal of the 30 days 195
- Your setup (do this on Day 1)..195
- Your weekly rhythm 196
- Week 1: Build foundations and clarity...197
- Week 2: Build community and conversation 197
- Week 3: Build offers and lead flow 198
- Week 4: Build advocacy and repeat visibility.....................................199
- Appendix B: Weekly content calendar template (copy and fill)....................199
- Appendix C: Content pillar planner and idea bank 200

PILLAR PLANNER (COPY) 200
IDEA BANK (TOP 30 PROMPTS) 201
APPENDIX D: CAPTION FORMULAS AND CALL-TO-ACTION BANK 202
CAPTION FORMULAS 202
CALL-TO-ACTION BANK 202
APPENDIX E: HASHTAG WORKSHEET (INCLUDING MOVEMENT HASHTAG SETUP) 203
HASHTAG CATEGORIES 203
HASHTAG WORKSHEET (COPY) 204
MOVEMENT HASHTAG SETUP STEPS 204
APPENDIX F: COMMUNITY RULES AND MODERATION SCRIPTS 204
COMMUNITY RULES (COPY AND EDIT) 204
MODERATION SCRIPTS 205
APPENDIX G: CUSTOMER MESSAGE TEMPLATES (DM REPLIES, ORDER CONFIRMATION, FOLLOW-UP) 205
APPENDIX H: SIMPLE ANALYTICS SHEET AND MONTHLY REVIEW TEMPLATE 206
WEEKLY SCORECARD (COPY) 206
MONTHLY REVIEW TEMPLATE (COPY) 206
APPENDIX I: LOW-DATA CREATION TIPS FOR LIMITED INTERNET ENVIRONMENTS 207
APPENDIX J: GLOSSARY OF KEY SOCIAL MEDIA MARKETING TERMS 207

BACK MATTER 209

FINAL NOTE TO THE READER 209
LEAVE A REVIEW (THREE PROMPTS) 211
ORDER AND BULK COPIES 211
ABOUT THE AUTHOR 212

DEDICATION

To every small business owner, creator, student, and worker who is trying to be seen in a noisy world without losing their soul.

To the people building with weak internet, limited tools, and strong courage.

And to those who believe that dignity, truth, and service can still win online.

ACKNOWLEDGMENTS

This book comes from watching people build real businesses in real conditions. I am grateful to the friends, clients, and learners who allowed me to observe their wins and mistakes up close. I am also grateful to the readers who keep reminding me of one simple truth: clarity is kindness. When I explain marketing in plain language, more people rise.

DISCLAIMER

This book is education, not legal, financial, medical, or tax advice. Social media platforms change often. Features, rules, and algorithms can shift without notice. I will teach principles that stay useful, plus practical steps you can adjust when platforms change. Results vary. Your outcome depends on your offer, your market, your consistency, your skill, and your ability to learn from feedback. Any names, scenes, or characters used in story sections are teaching examples unless I clearly state otherwise. I use examples to make lessons easy to remember, not to expose anyone.

A NOTE ABOUT THE STORY THREAD

I teach using a simple method: story first, lesson second, action third.
Sometimes I will show a scene where I am learning a hard truth, and someone like Nyakor pushes me to think differently. That is not just entertainment. It is how real learning happens. We resist, we argue, we test, and we change.
If you do not like stories, you can still use this book. After each story section, I translate the message into steps you can apply.

HOW TO USE THIS BOOK

Read one chapter, then do the action steps before you move to the next one.
If you rush, you will feel motivated but you will not build a system.
If you apply, even slowly, you will build a presence that lasts.

Here is my suggested rhythm:

First pass
Read the chapter in one sitting. Underline anything that feels true or challenging.
Write one sentence: what is the main lesson for me.

Second pass
Do the chapter exercises with real answers, not ideal answers.
Create the small asset for that chapter. A bio rewrite. A content plan. A DM script. A tracking sheet.

Third pass
Publish. Engage. Review.
Social media rewards action. If you only learn, you will stay invisible.

If your internet is weak
Batch work when you have stable connection. Write captions offline. Edit photos offline. Save drafts.
When you get a good signal, schedule posts, upload reels, and respond to comments in one focused session.

WHO THIS BOOK IS FOR

This book is for you if:
You are building a business, brand, ministry, project, or personal platform and you need attention that turns into trust
You post often but you do not see results, or you do not know why results rise and fall
You want to grow without copying people or using tricks that embarrass you

You want a simple way to plan content, talk with people, and track what works

This book is not for you if:
You are looking for shortcuts, fake followers, or spam tactics
You want promises of fast money without work
You refuse to reply to people, learn, and adjust

WHAT I WILL HELP YOU BUILD

By the end of this book, you will be able to:
Describe your brand in clear words that people understand fast
Create content that earns reach, saves, replies, and inquiries
Build a community that feels human, not like a crowd
Turn conversations into customers without pushing people
Track results, learn from numbers, and improve month after month

MY PROMISE AS YOUR GUIDE

I will not teach you hype.
I will not teach you manipulation.
I will teach you practical marketing that respects people.

I believe attention is rented, but trust is earned.
So we will focus on trust. Because trust survives algorithm changes.

TOOLS YOU NEED

You do not need expensive gear to start.
You need:
A phone with a decent camera
A note app for writing captions
A basic photo editor if you want it, but it is optional
A simple calendar for planning
A small notebook or spreadsheet for tracking results

If you have more tools, good. If you have less, we will still work with what you have.

ABOUT THE AUTHOR

My name is Panyim, John.

I write and teach about visibility, business building, and the discipline of showing up online with integrity. I have seen people with great products fail because nobody knew they existed. I have also seen ordinary products win because the owner built trust, told the truth, and served a community with consistency.

I believe social media marketing is not about being loud. It is about being clear. It is about helping the right people find you, understand you, and feel safe buying from you.

This book is my teaching guide, built for real life, built for people who want results and still want to sleep with a clean conscience.

PART ONE: THE POWER OF SOCIAL CONNECTION

Social media is not a poster wall. It is not a slot machine where you pull a handle and hope the algorithm smiles at you.

It is a public meeting place.

It is where trust is built in front of other people. It is where reputation becomes visible. And when you learn to use it with discipline, it becomes a bridge between your work and the people who need it.

I want you to read this first part with one big idea in your mind:

If people do not know you exist, they cannot buy from you, refer you, partner with you, hire you, or defend your name when lies spread.

A good product is not enough. A good service is not enough. Being talented is not enough.

Visibility creates opportunity. But visibility without integrity creates disaster.

So in this part, I start from the ground, from human behavior, from how people talk, share, trust, and buy. I will show you why social media matters, how community changes everything, and how knowing your audience turns posting into real marketing.

Now, let us begin.

Chapter One: Why social media matters
Story thread

I used to believe something that sounds innocent but is deadly in business.

"If the product is good, people will naturally find it."

One afternoon, I sat with Nyakor outside a small shop. We were not in a fancy office. We were just watching people pass. Some were rushing. Some were laughing. Some were looking at their phones like the phones were giving them oxygen.

I had my phone too. I was checking my page.

I had posted a photo of something I was proud of. Clean work. Strong value. Fair price. I wrote a caption that I thought was clear. I waited for results.

Nothing.

A few likes from friends. No inquiries. No sales.

I told Nyakor, "I do not understand. The work is good."

She looked at me the way an older sister looks at a younger brother who thinks the world owes him a reward for effort.

She said, "John, your work is good. But who knows it exists?"

I tried to defend myself. "People will hear. Word spreads."

She shook her head. "Word spreads when there is a path. You are hiding and calling it humility."

That sentence hit me.

Hiding and calling it humility.

I stared at my phone again. My page was quiet. My posts were scattered. My bio was confusing. My pictures were not telling a clear story. I was basically whispering in a crowded market and wondering why nobody turned their head.

Nyakor continued.

"You are thinking like a craftsman who expects the village to find his hut. Social media is the road. People do not teleport. They walk on roads."

Then she did something simple.

She opened Instagram and showed me three pages.

The first page had average work, but strong visibility. Every day, the owner posted. Every day, the owner replied to comments. Every day, the owner showed behind the scenes. Customers were tagged. Testimonials were pinned. Even the highlights were organized like a small shop shelf.

The second page had good work, but no system. Random photos. No clear offer. No location. No instructions for ordering. Comments left unanswered for weeks.

The third page had great work, but almost no presence. The owner posted once in a long while, and disappeared. No proof, no story, no community.

Nyakor pointed at the first page.

"Tell me the truth. If you were a customer, who would you trust?"

I did not like the answer, but I knew it.

I would trust the visible one. Not because the work was best, but because the trust was visible.

Then she said, "Social media is not only attention. It is a public record. When people see proof again and again, they relax. When they see silence, they worry."

That was the day I stopped treating social media like decoration.

I started treating it like a responsibility.

Because I realized something else.

Every day I stayed invisible, someone else took the customer I could have served better.

Every day I refused to show up, someone less honest showed up instead.

And when honest people hide, the marketplace gets louder with noise.

So I asked Nyakor, "What do I do first?"

She smiled.

"We start with the truth. Then we build the habit."

What I teach
1) What social media really is

When people talk about social media, they often talk about apps. They talk about reels, hashtags, stories, followers, likes.

Those are tools, not the main thing.

Social media is modern word of mouth.

But it is stronger than old word of mouth because it does two things at the same time:

- It spreads what people say.
- It stores what people said.

That second part changes everything.

In the past, someone could recommend you in a conversation, and the conversation would vanish into air.

Now, the recommendation can stay on your page for years.

A comment saying "This service is reliable" becomes a public witness.

A tagged customer photo becomes proof.

A story highlight becomes a track record.

Even your replies to people become part of your reputation.

So social media is not only a megaphone.

It is also a public notebook of trust.

That is why it matters.

Because trust is the main currency in business.

People do not only buy what is "good."
They buy what feels safe.

They buy what feels understood.

They buy what seems consistent.

They buy what others have tested.

Your page is one of the places where safety is measured.

2) The difference between posting and marketing

A lot of people post. Very few people market.

Posting is publishing content.

Marketing is moving people toward a goal.

When I post, I might be expressing myself.

When I market, I am guiding the reader.

Marketing has direction.

Marketing has a clear next step.

Marketing has a listener in mind.

Marketing is not only "look at me."
Marketing is "this is for you, and here is what to do next."

Here are a few examples:

- Posting: "New product available."
- Marketing: "If you struggle with X, this solves it. Here is how to order."
- Posting: A random selfie.
- Marketing: A selfie that connects to a story and a lesson, leading to a relevant offer.
- Posting: A photo with no caption.
- Marketing: A photo with a clear message, proof, and an invite.

Marketing does not have to be loud. It does not have to be pushy.

But it must be intentional.

If you are serious about building results, you must stop posting randomly.

You must start marketing on purpose.

3) How people move from stranger to follower to buyer to advocate

Let me tell you the truth most people avoid.

People do not buy because you posted once.

People buy after repetition.

They buy after exposure.

They buy after trust.

This is the journey most people take, even if they do not say it out loud:

Stranger
They do not know you.

Aware
They have seen you once or twice.

Interested
They stop scrolling sometimes. They watch. They read. They save.

Engaged
They comment. They reply to a story. They send a DM. They ask a question.

Buyer
They purchase.

Repeat buyer
They return because the experience matched the promise.

Advocate
They recommend you publicly. They defend you. They bring others.

This is not magic.

This is human behavior.

Social media matters because it supports every stage of this journey:

- It introduces you to strangers.
- It reminds the aware people.
- It educates the interested people.
- It makes it easy for engaged people to reach you.
- It reduces fear for buyers.
- It gives repeat buyers reasons to return.
- It gives advocates a stage to speak.

If you do not build for this journey, you will feel like social media is random.

But when you build with this journey in mind, your work starts to make sense.

4) Choosing outcomes: what do you want social media to do?

Many people get stuck because they have no goal.

They say, "I want to grow."

Grow what?

Followers?
Reach?
Sales?
Email list?
Walk in traffic?
Brand reputation?
Partnerships?

Social media can serve different outcomes, and each outcome needs different content.

Here are five common outcomes I teach my readers to choose from:

Awareness
You want more people to know you exist.
You focus on reach, shares, and discoverability.

Leads
You want people to contact you.
You focus on DMs, inquiries, link clicks, calls, appointments, sign ups.

Sales
You want transactions.
You focus on offers, proof, scarcity used honestly, and clear ordering steps.

Repeat customers
You want retention.
You focus on customer care, follow up, and community belonging.

Referrals
You want word of mouth to multiply.
You focus on advocacy, testimonials, and customer spotlight.

If you try to chase all outcomes at once, you will confuse yourself and your audience.

Choose one main outcome for the next 30 days.

You can still have secondary benefits, but you need one focus.

Clarity multiplies effort.

5) The "visibility with integrity" rule

This is where many people fail.

They see what works for dishonest people and they copy it.

They buy fake followers.

They promise miracles.

They act rich when they are drowning.

They use guilt. They use pressure. They use drama.

They might gain attention, but they poison trust.

My rule is simple:

I want attention that I can carry with clean hands.

Visibility without integrity is a short road that ends in shame.

So here is what I do and what I want you to do:

- I do not lie.
- I do not beg.
- I do not spam people's inboxes.
- I do not guilt people into buying.
- I do not pretend results I do not have.
- I do not insult my audience's intelligence.

Instead:

- I show proof.
- I tell true stories.
- I teach clearly.
- I serve consistently.
- I invite people to take a next step.

This is slower than manipulation, but it lasts longer.

And when hard seasons come, integrity becomes your shield.

Because people forgive mistakes. They do not forgive betrayal.

My action steps

I do not want you to admire this chapter. I want you to use it.

So here are the first steps I teach, the same steps I had to do when Nyakor made me stop hiding.

Step 1: Define one clear business goal for the next 30 days

Pick ONE main goal. Write it in a way you can measure.

Here are strong examples:

- "Get 30 qualified inquiries through DMs in 30 days."
- "Generate 10 sales that are influenced by social media in 30 days."
- "Book 8 consultations in 30 days."
- "Increase website visits from social by 25 percent in 30 days."
- "Get 20 repeat customers to return this month through follow up content."

Here are weak examples:

- "Go viral."
- "Grow my page."
- "Be popular."

You do not build a business on vague dreams.

You build it on measurable action.

Your 30-day goal
Write it now:

- Goal:
- Why this goal matters:
- What offer or service this goal is connected to:
- How I will measure it:

If you cannot connect your goal to an offer, your goal is entertainment, not marketing.

Step 2: Pick one primary platform and one support platform

Most people fail because they scatter.

They post a little on five platforms and build nothing on any of them.

I prefer focus.

Primary platform
This is where you invest most of your energy.
This is where you build community and trust.

Support platform
This is where you recycle content or support discovery.

Here is a practical way to choose:

Choose your primary platform based on:

- Where your audience already spends time
- Where your product category performs well
- Where you can show proof easily
- Where you can keep up consistently

Choose your support platform based on:

- Ease of repurposing
- Extra discovery and search
- Your personal comfort level

Examples that work for many people:

- Instagram primary, Facebook support
- TikTok primary, Instagram support
- Facebook primary, WhatsApp support

- YouTube primary, Instagram support
- LinkedIn primary, X support

Do not choose based on what is trendy.

Choose based on what you can sustain.

Your platform decision
Write it:

- Primary platform:
- Support platform:
- Why I chose them:
- What I will stop doing for 30 days to protect focus:

Step 3: Set a simple baseline

If you do not measure before you start, you will not know what changed.

A baseline is not a prison. It is a starting line.

I keep it simple. I track only what connects to my goal.

Here is a baseline tracker you can copy.

Baseline checklist (today)

- Followers:
- Average reach per post (last 10 posts):
- Average comments per post (last 10 posts):
- Average saves or shares per post (last 10 posts, if visible):
- Average story replies per week:
- Inquiries per week (DMs, calls, messages):
- Sales influenced by social per week:

If your page is new and you have no data, that is still data.

It means you are at the beginning.

And that is fine.

What matters is that you will not stay blind.

Step 4: Write your "visibility statement" for the month

This is a short sentence that keeps you grounded.

It stops you from performing. It keeps you serving.

Here is mine in many seasons:

"I will show up daily with truth, proof, and care, so the right people can find me and trust me."

Write yours:

- My visibility statement:

Step 5: Build a 30-day action rhythm

Do not create a plan that requires superhuman energy.

Create a rhythm that fits your life.

Here is a rhythm I teach for most small businesses:

Daily (15 to 30 minutes)

- Reply to comments
- Reply to DMs
- Post one story or one short update
- Leave 5 meaningful comments on other pages in your field

Three times per week

- Publish one main post (reel, carousel, or photo post with strong caption)

Once per week

- Review your numbers and write one lesson
- Update one highlight or pinned post

Once per month

- Review your goal and decide what to adjust

If your internet is weak, batch your content.

Write captions offline.
Save drafts.
Upload and schedule when the signal is stable.

Step 6: Create your "trust assets" first

Before you post more, make sure your page can answer basic questions.

When a stranger lands on your profile, they should quickly know:

- Who you are
- What you offer
- Where you are
- How to order or contact you
- Proof that you are real

Here is what I call your trust assets:

Profile

- Clear name
- Clear bio
- Clear offer
- Clear location
- Clear contact method

Pinned posts

- Start here
- Proof
- Offer

Highlights

- About
- Products or services
- Testimonials
- How to order
- FAQs

If these are missing, your page is like a shop with no signboard and no door.

A closing lesson before you move to Chapter Two

Social media matters because it turns invisible work into visible trust.

That is the whole game.

Not fame.
Not noise.

Trust.

When you build trust publicly, you do not need to chase customers like a hungry man chasing a running goat.

Customers come because the road is clear and the proof is visible.

In the next chapter, I will show you how to build community, not just an audience.

Because followers are numbers.

But community is strength.

Chapter Two: Building your online community
Story thread

I used to treat social media like a stall in a market.

I would show the product, name the price, and hope people bought.

Then Nyakor asked me a question that embarrassed me because it was simple.

"John, do you want customers or do you want people?"

I said, "Customers, of course. This is business."

She laughed, not to mock me, but to wake me up.

"You think customers arrive as customers. They do not. They arrive as people first."

That day, we walked through a real market. Not the digital one. The one where dust rises when people move and voices travel far.

Nyakor pointed at two sellers.

The first seller was loud. He shouted. He pulled people by the sleeve. He begged. He lowered prices like he was panicking. He had traffic, but his buyers looked tired.

The second seller was calm. People greeted him by name. A woman carried his product like it already belonged to her. A young man stopped just to chat. Buyers waited patiently.

I asked Nyakor, "What is the difference?"

She said, "The first one sells. The second one belongs."

Belongs.

That word stayed with me.

Later that evening, I opened my page and saw the truth.

I had followers, but I had no belonging.

I had likes, but I had no culture.

I had posts, but I had no shared identity.

My page was a billboard, not a village.

So I asked Nyakor, "How do I make people belong online?"

She took my phone, looked at my bio, and said, "First you stop talking like a seller. You start talking like a builder."

Then she wrote a sentence on a piece of paper.

Not a long paragraph. One sentence.

"This page is for people who want to build a meaningful life through work, culture, and integrity."

She gave me the paper and said, "That is your community promise. That is what people join."

I stared at it. It sounded too simple.

But she continued.

"Now we need a gathering point. A sign. A name. A hashtag."

I had been using hashtags like decoration, like throwing sand into the air.

Nyakor told me to create one that meant something, one that carried identity.

She said, "A good hashtag is like a drumbeat. It calls people. It repeats. It creates memory."

So I created one and started using it with discipline.

At first, nothing changed.

Then something small happened.

A follower used my hashtag on their own post.

Then another.

Then someone sent me a message.

"John, I used your hashtag because your message makes more sense. I want to be part of this."

That was the first time I understood community online.

Not as an idea.

As a feeling.

People do not only want to buy.

People want to be seen.

They want to be included.

They want to belong to something that reflects their values.

And that is when my page stopped being a stall.

It started becoming a meeting place.

What I teach
Audience versus community

Many people chase an audience because numbers are easy to count.

Followers.
Views.
Likes.
Reach.

An audience is "people who watch."

A community is "people who belong."

Here is how I see it in real life.

An audience claps and goes home.

A community stays and helps clean the chairs.

An audience consumes.

A community contributes.

An audience asks, "What do you have for me?"

A community asks, "How can we build this together?"

If you only build an audience, your growth will feel fragile.

Because when the algorithm changes, your attention can collapse.

But when you build community, you build a base that survives shifts.

Because community is carried by people, not by a platform.

Community is what makes your followers defend you when lies spread.

Community is what makes buyers return even when competitors appear.

Community is what makes people share your work without you begging.

So my first lesson is this:

Stop thinking like a performer. Start thinking like a host.

A performer is trying to be liked.

A host is trying to gather people and serve them well.

When you host well, people return.

How to recognize what you have right now

Ask yourself these questions. Answer honestly.

- Do people reply to my stories without being forced?
- Do people tag me when they use my product or apply my ideas?
- Do people ask questions that show trust?
- Do people return to comment again and again?
- Do people defend my work when someone mocks it?
- Do people use my words, my phrases, my hashtag?

If the answer is mostly no, you do not have community yet.

You have visibility.

And that is not shameful. It is simply the starting point.

Community is built, not wished into existence.

How a simple hashtag becomes a rally point

Most people use hashtags as a fishing net.

Throw many tags, hope you catch something.

That approach can work for reach, but it rarely builds belonging.

A rally point hashtag does something different.

It signals identity.

It says, "If you feel this message, you are one of us."

Think of it as a flag, not a net.

Not a flag for pride.

A flag for shared values.

What makes a rally point hashtag strong

A strong rally point hashtag is:

- Short enough to remember
- Easy to spell
- Unique enough that it is not drowned by millions of unrelated posts
- Close to your message, not random
- Emotional, not technical

It also has a job.

It is not there to decorate your caption.

It is there to gather posts into one visible place.

When people click it, they should see a world that makes sense.

Not confusion.

Not noise.

A world.

Two kinds of hashtags you should use

I teach two types of hashtags and I separate them on purpose.

1) Discovery hashtags
These help strangers find you.
They are more general.

Examples:
#southsudanbusiness
#handmadefashion
#digitalnomadlife
#smallbusinessmarketing

2) Community hashtags
These help your people gather.
They are more specific.
Often branded.

Examples:
#BuildWithIntegrity
#MeaningfulWorkMovement
#PanmalPeaceBuilders
#PanyimBuildersCircle

The discovery hashtags bring strangers.

The community hashtag turns strangers into members.

Many creators do the first and forget the second.

So they grow followers, but they do not grow belonging.

How I introduce a community hashtag without sounding fake

I do not announce it like a corporation.

I attach it to a meaning.

I tell a story and then I name the rally point.

For example, I might write:

"I am building for people who want results without selling their values. If you are one of us, use [HASHTAG] when you share your work so we can find each other."

That is enough.

The key is discipline.

A hashtag works when you keep using it and keep responding to the people who use it.

If you abandon it, it dies.

A rally point must be kept alive like a fire.

Creating participation loops: ask, feature, respond, repeat

Community does not grow because you post.

Community grows because people participate.

Participation is not an accident.

Participation is designed.

This is the simplest loop I know that works across almost every platform:

Ask → Feature → Respond → Repeat

Let me break it down in plain language.

Ask

You invite people to do something.

Not "like and share."

Something real.

Something that costs a little effort.

Examples:

- "Show me your work setup today."
- "Post your biggest challenge this week and I will reply with one practical step."
- "Share one habit you are building this month."
- "Use our hashtag and show your progress."

The best asks are specific.

If you ask vague questions, you get silence.

Feature

When someone participates, you spotlight them.

You repost their story.
You pin their comment.
You mention their name.
You celebrate their progress.

Featuring is powerful because it says, "You are seen."

People do not forget being seen.

Respond

You reply.

You do not just repost and disappear.

You talk back.

You answer questions.

You say thank you.

You correct mistakes kindly.

You add value.

This is where many people fail.

They want community, but they do not want the work of conversation.

You cannot build belonging without replies.

Repeat

You do it again, consistently.

Not once.

Not once when you feel inspired.

Weekly is enough to start.

Consistency trains people to expect the gathering.

Like a weekly market day.

Like a Sunday service.

Like a monthly family meeting.

If your participation loop is reliable, community starts to form around it.

User-generated content as proof and as fuel

User-generated content is when your followers create content about your work.

They post your product.
They share your quote.
They show your method in action.
They tag you.
They use your hashtag.

Many business owners treat this like a bonus.

I treat it like gold.

Because user-generated content does two things at once:

Proof
It shows that real people trust you, buy from you, or apply your lessons.

Fuel
It becomes content you can share, which saves you time and increases reach.

But there is a deeper reason it matters.

When people create content about your brand, they are not just consuming.

They are investing identity.

They are saying, "This is part of who I am."

That is how community becomes strong.

How to earn user-generated content without begging

Begging looks like this:

"Please post me. Please tag me. Please promote me."

Earning looks like this:

- You deliver a great experience.
- You make it easy to share.
- You publicly appreciate people who share.
- You create rituals that invite sharing.

Here are practical ways I earn it.

1) Make sharing easy
Give people simple prompts:

- "If you bought this, post a photo and tag me."
- "If you used this tip, share your result and use our hashtag."

2) Reward with recognition
Not money. Recognition.

People like to be seen.

Repost their story.
Thank them publicly.

3) Teach people what to share
Many people want to support you but do not know how.

Tell them:

- "Share a photo."

- "Share a before and after."
- "Share a short review."
- "Share a clip of you using it."

4) Protect their dignity
If you repost someone, do it respectfully.

Do not twist their message.
Do not embarrass them.
Do not use their image for jokes.

Trust grows when people feel safe.

Basic permission rule

In many cases, when someone tags you, they expect you to share.

Still, I prefer to build a habit of asking in a simple way.

"Thank you for sharing. May I repost this?"

That sentence builds respect.

And respect builds community.

Community guidelines and healthy moderation from day one

If you build a gathering, you will eventually face conflict.

Not because you did something wrong.

Because humans arrive with pain, pride, and differences.

A strong community is not one that has no conflict.

A strong community is one that handles conflict without poisoning the space.

This is why guidelines matter.

Guidelines are not control.

Guidelines are protection.

They protect the people who come in good faith.

They protect the tone of the space.

They protect your reputation.

What I include in community guidelines

I keep it simple and clear.

I do not write a long list that nobody reads.

I post guidelines in a highlight, in a pinned post, or occasionally in a story.

Here are the core rules I recommend for most brands.

Respect
No insults. No mocking people. No tribal or racist attacks. No religious hate. No gender hate.

No spam
No dropping links without permission. No begging for follows in the comments. No selling in my space unless allowed.

Protect privacy
No posting private information. No exposing other people.

Debate is allowed, abuse is not
You can disagree, but you cannot dehumanize.

My page, my house
I moderate to protect the community. I remove what damages the space.

That is enough.

Healthy moderation habits

Here is how I moderate without becoming a dictator.

1) Set the tone with your own behavior
If you reply with respect, your community learns respect.
If you reply with sarcasm and humiliation, your community learns cruelty.

2) Remove poison early
A small insult can grow into a war if you let it sit.

Delete.
Hide.
Block.

You do not owe everyone a platform in your space.

3) Do not argue with trolls
A troll wants attention, not truth.

I either ignore or remove them.

If the comment can confuse my audience, I reply once with calm clarity, then I stop.

4) Protect the vulnerable
If someone shares a struggle, do not allow mockery.

People must feel safe to be honest.

5) Create a simple escalation ladder
I use a three-step ladder:

- Warning (only if the person seems genuine)
- Delete or hide
- Block

If the person is clearly abusive, I skip steps.

What to do when conflict is between members

When two followers fight in your comments, do not pretend you did not see it.

You are the host.

Here is my approach:

- I remind them of guidelines.
- I remove insults.
- I invite them to take it to private messages if it is personal.
- If they refuse, I block.

Your community learns from what you tolerate.

If you tolerate disrespect, you are teaching disrespect.

My action steps

Now I want you to build your community foundation.

Not next month.

Now.

These steps are designed to be done in one focused day, and then maintained weekly.

Action step 1: Create your community promise in one sentence

A community promise is your "why" made simple.

It tells people what they are joining.

It also helps you stay consistent.

A strong community promise has three parts:

- Who it is for
- What it stands for
- What kind of experience people will have

Here are examples you can adapt.

If you are a small business
"This page is for people who value quality, honesty, and local craftsmanship, and we gather here to support each other through meaningful buying."

If you are a coach or teacher
"This page is for people building skills and discipline, and we gather here to learn, practice, and grow without shame."

If you are a creator
"This page is for people who love culture and stories, and we gather here to celebrate identity and create work that lasts."

Now write yours.

Bold it. Make it clear. Make it human.

Your community promise
Write one sentence:

- "This page is for _____, and we gather here to _____."

After you write it, test it.

Ask:
Does this feel true?
Would I join this?
Can I keep this promise?

If you cannot keep it, rewrite it.

Do not promise what you cannot deliver.

Action step 2: Design a unique hashtag that fits your message and is easy to remember

You are going to create one community hashtag.

Not 20.

One.

Here is my process.

Step A: Choose the core theme

Pick one theme from your community promise.

Examples:

- integrity
- discipline
- culture
- peace
- growth
- craftsmanship
- learning
- family
- faith
- entrepreneurship

Step B: Add a gathering word

Use words that signal "we" and "together."

Examples:

- circle
- builders
- tribe (use carefully depending on your audience)
- movement
- community
- family
- crew
- team
- collective

Step C: Combine them into a clean hashtag

Aim for:
Short
Readable
No weird spelling
No confusing punctuation
No numbers unless necessary

Examples:

- #IntegrityBuilders
- #CultureAndCraft
- #DisciplineCircle
- #PeaceBuilders
- #MeaningfulWorkCircle

Step D: Check uniqueness

Search it on the platform.

If it is full of unrelated posts, adjust it.

Add your name, brand, or a unique word.

Examples:

- #PanyimIntegrityBuilders
- #PanmalPeaceBuilders

Step E: Write your hashtag meaning

Do not assume people will "get it."

Write one simple sentence you can reuse:

"We use [HASHTAG] to share our progress and find each other."

That is it.

Now write yours.

Your community hashtag

- Hashtag:
- Meaning sentence:

Action step 3: Plan a weekly participation ritual

If you do not create a rhythm, you will rely on motivation.

Motivation is unreliable.

A ritual is stronger.

A ritual is a repeated gathering that trains community behavior.

Choose ONE ritual for the next 4 weeks.

Here are four options that work well.

Option 1: Weekly challenge

A small task people can do and share.

Examples:

- "Show your workspace."
- "Post your weekly goal."
- "Share one improvement you made."
- "Show your product in use."

How to run it:

- Announce the challenge on the same day each week.
- Ask people to use the hashtag.
- Feature 3 to 10 people who participate.
- Thank them publicly.

Option 2: Weekly prompt

A question that invites story.

Examples:

- "What was your hardest lesson this week?"
- "What are you building right now?"
- "What are you learning that changed your thinking?"
- "What does integrity mean in your work today?"

How to run it:

- Post the prompt as a story and a post.
- Reply to answers.
- Pin one powerful answer.
- Summarize the best answers at the end of the week.

Option 3: Weekly spotlight

You feature a community member.

Examples:

- customer of the week
- follower of the week
- student of the week
- maker of the week

How to run it:

- Ask permission.
- Share their photo and short story.
- Tag them.
- Invite others to participate.

This builds belonging fast.

Option 4: Weekly live session

A short live, even 15 minutes.

Examples:

- Q and A
- teaching one skill
- behind the scenes
- reviewing community posts

How to run it:

- Use a consistent day and time.
- Collect questions beforehand.
- Save the live and pin it if possible.

Now choose one.

Your weekly ritual

- Ritual type:
- Day of week:

- Time:
- What people do:
- What you will feature:
- How you will respond:

Action step 4: Write your "participation script"

This is what you say every week so people understand the system.

Copy this structure and adjust it:

Invitation
"Today is our community day."

Action
"Here is what to do: [specific task]."

Tag
"Use [HASHTAG] and tag me so I can see it."

Reward
"I will repost my favorites and highlight a few people."

Belonging
"This is how we grow together."

Keep it short.

People do not need poetry.

They need clarity.

Action step 5: Create your community guidelines in five lines

Write five lines.

Post them in a highlight or pinned post.

Example:

- Respect people. No insults or hate.
- No spam or link dumping.
- Debate is allowed. Abuse is not.
- Protect privacy. Do not expose others.
- I moderate to keep this space healthy.

Now write yours:

Your guidelines

- Line 1:
- Line 2:
- Line 3:
- Line 4:
- Line 5:

Action step 6: Build your "UGC request" message

You will need a simple message you send to happy customers or engaged followers.

Here is a template you can reuse.

"Thank you for supporting my work. If you are comfortable, please share a photo or short note about your experience, tag me, and use [HASHTAG]. It helps others trust, and it helps our community grow. If you share, may I repost it?"

That message is respectful, clear, and human.

Extra teaching: how I keep community from becoming exhausting

Community can drain you if you do it without boundaries.

So I use three rules.

Rule 1: I schedule engagement

I do not reply all day.

I pick windows.

Example:

- morning: 20 minutes
- evening: 20 minutes

If you reply randomly all day, you will feel trapped.

If you reply in windows, you will feel in control.

Rule 2: I do not let community replace my life

Community is a tool, not a god.

I will serve, but I will not drown.

This is important because many creators burn out and then disappear.

Disappearing breaks trust.

So protect your energy.

Rule 3: I build systems that do not require my constant presence

That is why rituals matter.

That is why highlights matter.

That is why pinned posts matter.

Systems keep the house running even when the host is tired.

Closing message for this chapter

If you only sell, you will always be chasing.

If you build community, you will start being carried.

Not carried by magic.

Carried by people who feel seen, respected, and included.

Your community promise tells people why they should stay.

Your hashtag gives them a place to gather.

Your participation loop gives them a reason to contribute.

Your guidelines protect the space.

This is how a page becomes more than content.

It becomes belonging.

Chapter Three: Understanding your audience
Story thread

I used to say, "My business is for everyone."

I said it with pride, like I was being generous.

Nyakor did not argue with me. She just asked one question.

"If it is for everyone, then who is it for when you wake up tomorrow morning?"

I did not have an answer.

That night, I opened my page and scrolled through my posts. They looked like a person throwing stones into a river and hoping fish jump out.

One post sounded like I was speaking to students.
Another post sounded like I was speaking to rich customers.
Another post sounded like I was speaking to friends.
Another post sounded like I was speaking to nobody.

Nyakor told me, "You are not failing because your work is weak. You are failing because your message is scattered."

The next day, she asked me to sit with her and do something I avoided.

Listen.

Not talk. Not post. Not explain myself.

Listen.

She said, "Open your DMs. Read them slowly. Do not reply yet."

I saw messages I had ignored or answered too fast.

"How much is it?"
"Do you deliver?"
"Can I pay later?"
"Is this original?"
"Do you have a smaller size?"
"Can you make one with this color?"
"Where are you located?"
"Do you do custom work?"
"I want something that shows who I am."

Nyakor stopped me at that last message.

"I want something that shows who I am."

She asked me, "Did you see it?"

I said, "See what?"

She said, "People are not buying your product. They are buying what it does for their identity."

That was the first moment I understood the real work of marketing.

Marketing is not talking louder.

Marketing is hearing deeper.

Nyakor took my notebook and drew two simple columns:

Real fan
Real buyer

She said, "List names. Real names. People you know."

I wrote down the names of those who always liked my posts, always praised me, always commented "Great work," but never bought.

Then I wrote down the names of those who rarely liked anything, rarely commented, but bought quietly, sometimes multiple times, and referred others.

Nyakor pointed at the list and said, "Now you see it. The fan and the buyer are not always the same person."

Then she said something that changed how I create content.

"You are posting for applause. But you need to post for action."

That day, I stopped trying to speak to everyone.

I started trying to serve specific people with specific needs.

And when I did that, my content became simpler, clearer, and more effective.

Because a market is not a crowd.

A market is a group of people with a shared problem or desire.

What I teach
1) How I identify the real buyer and the real fan

If you want consistent results, you must understand two groups:

The people who enjoy you
The people who pay you

Both matter, but they are not the same.

A real fan is someone who:

- Engages often
- Shares your content
- Comments and encourages you
- Promotes your message

- Helps your reach grow

A real buyer is someone who:

- Has the problem your offer solves
- Has the desire your offer fulfills
- Has money or access to money
- Is ready to act
- Trusts you enough to risk a purchase

Here is the key:

Fans increase visibility.
Buyers increase revenue.

You need both, but your marketing must not confuse them.

If you only chase fans, you will build popularity without profit. If you only chase buyers, you might sell, but you will struggle to grow reach and trust.

So what do I do?

I separate my content into two purposes:

Some content is for fans, to spread and build community. Some content is for buyers, to answer objections and drive inquiries.

I also stop assuming the loudest people are the best customers.

Sometimes the best customers are silent.

They watch. They evaluate. Then they buy.

Practical way to identify your buyers:

- Look at who has paid you in the last 90 days

- Look at who has referred others
- Look at who asks serious questions (delivery, payment, timeline, details)
- Look at who returns

Practical way to identify your fans:

- Look at who comments consistently
- Look at who saves and shares
- Look at who defends your work in public

When you can name these groups, you can create content that respects both.

2) The jobs people hire my product for

People do not buy products. They buy outcomes.

They hire your product to do a job in their life.

This idea is powerful because it stops you from guessing.

Instead of asking, "What should I post today?"
You ask, "What job do people hire my offer for, and how do I show that?"

Here are common jobs people hire products and services for.

Status
People buy to signal success or taste.
Example: "This shows I have arrived."

Identity
People buy to express who they are.
Example: "This feels like me."

Convenience
People buy to save time or reduce stress.
Example: "This makes my life easier."

Belonging
People buy to feel included in a group.
Example: "This connects me to my people."

Gifting
People buy to honor someone else.
Example: "This is how I show love."

Problem-solving
People buy to fix a pain.
Example: "This removes a struggle."

Your job is to discover which of these jobs are most common for your offer.

Then build content that proves you can deliver.

If you sell a service, the jobs still apply.
If you sell teaching, the jobs still apply.
If you sell products, the jobs still apply.

Once you know the job, your content stops being random.

It becomes targeted.

3) Simple audience research inside the apps

You do not need a university lab to understand your audience.

Your audience is already telling you what they want every day.

The problem is that most creators do not listen with intention.

Here are simple research methods I use inside the apps.

Comments
Comments reveal:

- what people agree with
- what confuses them
- what triggers them
- what they want more of

I screenshot comments that show strong emotion or strong clarity. Then I build content from them.

DMs
DMs reveal:

- buying intent
- hidden fears
- real questions people are afraid to ask publicly
- the language people use when they describe their need

DMs are not only messages. They are market research.

Polls
Polls are a fast way to test what matters.

Good poll questions are specific.
Bad poll questions are vague.

Good:
"Do you struggle more with posting ideas or consistency?"
"Which is harder for you: writing captions or making videos?"
"What would you rather learn next: pricing or promotion?"

Story replies
Story replies are a gold mine because they are private and honest.

People will confess in story replies more than in comments.

I use stories to ask:

- what they are working on
- what they fear
- what they want next

- what they tried that failed

The key is to document what you learn.

If you do not write it down, you will forget and keep guessing.

4) How to build content pillars that match audience needs

Content pillars are the main themes you talk about repeatedly.

They keep your page consistent.
They train your audience to understand what you are about.
They make content creation easier.

Many people choose pillars based on what they like, not what the audience needs.

I choose pillars where these three things overlap:

- what my audience needs
- what I can deliver with credibility
- what connects to my offer

A strong set of pillars usually has 3 to 5 themes.

Here are examples.

If you sell a product:

- product education (what it is, how it works)
- behind the scenes (how it is made, quality proof)
- customer stories (testimonials, use cases)
- lifestyle and identity (how it fits their life)
- offers and ordering (how to buy, what is available)

If you are a service provider:

- problem education (the pain you solve)

- process proof (how you work, what clients can expect)
- results and case studies
- FAQs and objections (pricing, timing, trust)
- offers and calls to action

If you are a teacher:

- teaching content (how to do the thing)
- mindset and discipline (how to stay consistent)
- stories and examples (proof you have lived it)
- tools and templates (practical help)
- invitation (program, book, coaching, consultation)

Once your pillars are clear, your audience stops being confused.

And when the audience is not confused, buying becomes easier.

Confusion kills conversion.

My action steps

Now I want you to do the work that makes the next chapters easier.

Do these steps with honesty, not fantasy.

Step 1: Write 3 audience groups you serve, with one pain point and one desire each

Choose three groups only.

Not ten.

Three.

Each group should feel real, like you can picture them.

Use this structure:

Audience group 1
Who they are:
Pain point:
Desire:

Audience group 2
Who they are:
Pain point:
Desire:

Audience group 3
Who they are:
Pain point:
Desire:

Example (adjust to your world):

Audience group 1
Who they are: busy professionals
Pain point: no time to shop or compare options
Desire: convenience and reliability

Audience group 2
Who they are: young creatives
Pain point: they want to stand out but feel ignored
Desire: identity and status

Audience group 3
Who they are: gift buyers
Pain point: they do not know what is meaningful
Desire: gifting that feels personal

When you finish, ask:
Which group is most likely to buy in the next 30 days?

That group should shape your next month of content.

Step 2: Build a question bank for polls, captions, and lives

A question bank saves you from daily confusion.

Write at least 20 questions, but start with 10 if you are tired.

Use three categories:

Research questions (to learn)
Engagement questions (to start conversation)
Buyer questions (to move people toward action)

Examples:

Research:
"What is your biggest struggle with X?"
"What have you tried that did not work?"

Engagement:
"What is one win you had this week?"
"What are you building right now?"

Buyer:
"What would stop you from buying this today?"
"Do you prefer delivery or pickup?"

Write yours and keep them in a note app.

When you do not know what to post, open the bank.

Step 3: Create a "top 20 topics" list and reuse it across formats

This is how you stop feeling like content is endless labor.

You do not need endless ideas.

You need reusable themes.

Write 20 topics that match your content pillars.

Topic examples:

- pricing and value
- quality proof
- how to order
- behind the scenes
- before and after
- common mistakes
- customer spotlight
- FAQ answers
- product care tips
- how it fits identity and lifestyle

Now write your top 20.

Then reuse them across formats:

A topic can become:

- a reel
- a carousel
- a story series
- a live session
- a post with a strong caption
- a customer spotlight

This is how serious marketers stay consistent.

They do not search for new topics every day.

They go deeper on the same useful themes.

Closing lesson for this chapter

When you try to speak to everyone, you speak to nobody.

When you choose a real audience, your words become sharper.

Your message becomes easier to understand.
Your content becomes easier to create.
Your offers become easier to sell.

Listen before you post.

Your audience is already telling you what they want.

Your job is to pay attention, write it down, and serve them with discipline.

PART TWO: CRAFTING YOUR SOCIAL MEDIA PRESENCE

There is a moment in business when you realize that quality alone is silent.

Quality does not introduce itself.

Quality does not walk into rooms and explain its purpose.

Quality does not remove doubts from the mind of a stranger.

You must give it a voice.

But not a voice that sounds like begging.
Not a voice that sounds like performance.

A human voice.

In Part One, I taught you that social media is modern word of mouth and a public record of trust. I also taught you how to build community and how to understand the real people you serve. Now Part Two is about what those people see when they meet you online.

This is where many businesses lose customers without realizing it.

They post good content, but their profile is confusing.
They have a good product, but their story feels fake.
They are talented, but their voice sounds like everyone else.
They have values, but their page does not show those values.

In this part, I will teach you how I craft a social presence that feels clear, trustworthy, memorable, and rooted. Your presence is not only your posts. It is your identity expressed in public.

Now let us begin with the foundation.

Chapter Four: A compelling brand story
Story thread

I used to hate "branding."

Not because I did not understand it, but because I misunderstood it.

I thought branding meant acting like a corporation.

I thought it meant polished slogans, big claims, and a shiny image that does not match reality.

So I avoided it.

I posted my work and expected people to understand.

Then one day, Nyakor showed me what strangers see when they land on my profile.

She took my phone and said, "John, look at this as if you do not know you."

She read my bio out loud.

It was full of words, but empty of meaning.

It said things like "quality," "best," "professional," and "service."

Nyakor paused and asked, "Best for who?"

I shrugged.

She opened my highlights.

Random.

No order. No story. No proof.

She opened my pinned posts.

There were none.

She then scrolled my feed.

It was not terrible, but it did not feel like a person. It felt like a seller.

Nyakor looked at me and said, "Your work may be honest, but your page does not prove it."

That sentence stung.

Because I knew I was honest.

But the internet cannot feel your heart.

The internet reads what you show.

That day, Nyakor gave me a challenge.

"Explain your brand in one minute without selling."

I started talking like I was in a marketplace.

I said the prices.
I said the features.
I said the product names.

She stopped me.

"John, that is not a story. That is a list."

Then she asked me three questions:

"Who do you serve?"
"What do you change for them?"
"Why do you care?"

I started answering slowly.

I talked about the people I grew up with, people who worked hard but stayed invisible.
I talked about how dignity matters, how work should not be hidden, how people deserve to be seen.
I talked about why integrity mattered to me, because I had seen what lies do to communities and families.

Nyakor nodded.

She said, "That is your story. That is your brand. Not the product list."

Then she said something that surprised me:

"Your roots are not a weakness. Your roots are your advantage."

I had been trying to sound global by sounding like everyone.

Nyakor told me to sound like myself.

To tell the truth.
To speak clearly.
To stop exaggerating.
To stop trying to impress strangers.

She said, "People do not remember perfect. People remember real."

So we rebuilt my presence around a story that felt human.

Not polished.
Not desperate.
Not fake.

Human.

And the strange thing is, when I did that, I did not become less professional.

I became more trustworthy.

Because trust is not built by big claims.

Trust is built by clear truth repeated over time.

What I teach
1) The three parts of my brand story

A brand story is not a biography.

It is not every detail of your life.

It is a simple explanation of why you exist in the market and why people should care.

I build my brand story using three parts.

Who I serve
This is the person I am for.

Not "everyone."
Not "all people."
A real group.

Examples:

- busy parents who want reliable services
- young professionals who want a clean look and confidence
- small business owners who want visibility without shame
- students who want skills that lead to work

What I change for them
This is the outcome.

Not the feature.
Not the process.

The result.

Examples:

- I help you save time and stress
- I help you look professional and feel confident
- I help you build consistent online visibility
- I help you turn confusion into a simple system

Why I care
This is the heart.

Why do you do this work?
What do you believe?

People connect to meaning.

When you explain why you care, the right people lean in.

Examples:

- because I grew up seeing honest work stay hidden
- because I believe dignity is part of prosperity
- because I have seen how manipulation destroys trust
- because I want people to build without losing themselves

When you combine these three parts, your story becomes clear.

It becomes easy to repeat.
Easy to remember.
Easy to trust.

Here is a simple formula you can reuse:

"I help (who) achieve (change) because (why)."

That is a brand story in one line.

2) Origin story without exaggeration

Many people ruin their brand story by exaggerating.

They claim they are the best.
They claim they are number one.
They claim results they cannot prove.

Exaggeration creates attention, but it also creates suspicion.

If your goal is trust, exaggeration is a slow poison.

Your origin story should answer one question:

Why did you start?

It does not need drama.
It does not need tears.
It does not need fake struggle.

It needs truth.

A strong origin story includes:

- a real problem you saw
- a moment you decided to act
- the lesson you learned
- the promise you now live by

Here is an example structure:

"I started because I noticed _____.
I saw that people struggled with _____.

I learned that _____.
Now I do _____ for people who want _____."

Your origin story does not have to be long.

In social media, short stories win because attention is limited.

But short does not mean shallow.

Short means focused.

The key rule:
Tell only what supports your brand promise.

Do not tell every detail of your life.
Tell the detail that explains your mission.

3) Brand voice: how I sound in captions, comments, and DMs

Your voice is not your logo.

Your voice is how you talk.

It is your tone, your rhythm, your values in language.

Many people have good products but lose trust because their voice feels artificial.

They sound like they copied someone else.
They sound like a script.
They sound like a bot.

Your voice should feel like one person, not a committee.

Here is how I define brand voice.

I choose 3 to 5 voice traits.

Examples:

- clear
- respectful
- direct
- warm
- confident
- humble
- bold
- calm

Then I apply them everywhere:

- captions
- comments
- DMs
- story text
- offers

If your captions sound formal, but your DMs sound rude, trust breaks.
If your posts sound kind, but your comments are arrogant, trust breaks.

Voice consistency is a hidden weapon.

It makes your brand feel stable.

Here is how I keep my voice stable:

- I write like I speak.
- I avoid fancy words I do not use in real life.
- I do not pretend to be rich or perfect.
- I talk to people like humans, not like numbers.

Your voice should fit your personality and your audience.

If your audience is youth, your voice can be more casual.
If your audience is corporate, your voice can be more structured.
But in all cases, your voice must feel human.

4) Profile setup that sells without sounding desperate

Your profile is your storefront.

Most people think the feed sells.

No.

The profile sells first.

A stranger lands on your profile and decides in seconds: stay or leave.

So I set up my profile like this.

Bio
A strong bio answers:

- who I am
- who I help
- what I offer
- where I am
- how to contact or order

Avoid empty words like "best" and "quality" without proof.

Use specific language.

Highlights
Highlights are your shelves.

I recommend these basic highlights for most businesses:

- Start here

- Products or services
- Proof or reviews
- How to order
- FAQs
- About

Keep them clean and organized.

Pinned posts
Pinned posts are your front door.

I use three pinned posts:

- Start here: my story, my promise, what people can expect
- Proof: testimonials, results, behind-the-scenes credibility
- Offer: what I sell and how to buy

This alone can transform a page.

Because strangers hate confusion.

Pinned posts reduce confusion.

Link strategy
One link is enough for many small businesses.

The key is to link to the next step that matches your goal.

Examples:

- WhatsApp link for orders
- website landing page
- booking calendar
- email signup page

Do not give people ten options.

Options create delay.
Delay kills action.

Make the next step obvious.

5) Cultural authenticity as a strength, not a limitation

Many people try to hide their roots online.

They think culture makes them look local and therefore "small."

That is a mistake.

Culture is what makes you memorable.

Culture is what makes you different.

Culture creates story.

But you must use culture with respect, not as costume.

Here is how I treat cultural authenticity:

- I speak from real experience, not borrowed identity.
- I honor where I come from without insulting others.
- I do not use culture to divide people.
- I use culture to show meaning, values, and belonging.

The internet is full of copycats.

Authenticity is what cannot be copied.

If you tell the truth about your roots, the right people will trust you more, not less.

Your roots become your signature.

My action steps

Now I want you to build the core assets of your presence.

Do not overthink.

Do the work.

Action step 1: Write my brand story in 50 words, then in 15 words

Start with 50 words.

Use the three parts:
who I serve, what I change, why I care.

Here is a template:

"I help _____ (who) to _____ (change) by _____ (how) because _____ (why)."

Now write it in 50 words.

Then compress it to 15 words.

The 15-word version is useful for:

- bio
- introductions
- live sessions
- networking

Example structure for 15 words:
"I help (who) achieve (change) through (method) because (why)."

Write both versions now:

50-word version:
15-word version:

Action step 2: Create 3 pinned posts: start here, proof, offer

Plan them before you design them.

Pinned post 1: Start here
Include:

- who I am
- who I serve
- what this page is about
- what to do next (follow, DM, link)

Pinned post 2: Proof
Include:

- testimonials
- before and after
- behind-the-scenes process
- numbers if you have them
- customer stories

Pinned post 3: Offer
Include:

- what I sell
- who it is for
- price range or how pricing works
- how to order
- delivery or pickup details
- contact method

Write the core message for each pinned post now.

Start here:
Proof:
Offer:

Action step 3: Draft 5 "about my work" story slides I can reuse monthly

Stories disappear fast, but you can reuse the same structure monthly.

Create five slides.

Keep them simple.
One idea per slide.

Here is a reusable set:

Slide 1: Who I am
"I am _____. I help _____."

Slide 2: What I believe
"I believe _____. That is why I do this work."

Slide 3: What I offer
"Here is what I offer: _____."

Slide 4: Proof
"Here is a recent result or review: _____."

Slide 5: Next step
"If you want this, send me a message with the word _____."

Now draft your own versions.

Slide 1:
Slide 2:
Slide 3:
Slide 4:
Slide 5:

Closing lesson for this chapter

A strong brand story does not shout.

It clarifies.

It tells the right people, "This is for you," and tells the wrong people, "This is not your place."

That is not rejection.

That is focus.

When your story is clear, your content becomes easier to create, your audience becomes easier to serve, and your offers become easier to sell.

In the next chapter, I will show you how to create engaging content that matches your brand story and moves people to action.

Chapter Five: Creating engaging content
Story thread

For a long time, I treated content like weather.

Some days I felt inspired, so I posted.
Some days I felt tired, so I disappeared.

When engagement went up, I felt proud.
When engagement went down, I felt angry.
I blamed the algorithm the way people blame rain.

Then Nyakor watched me struggle for weeks and said, "John, you are guessing."

I wanted to argue. I had been posting. I had been trying.

But she was right.

I was guessing about what to post.
Guessing about what people wanted.
Guessing about what worked.
Guessing about why something did well.

Nyakor told me, "Guessing is expensive. It costs time, energy, and confidence."

One afternoon she asked me to show her my last ten posts. We looked at them together, not like creators, but like strangers.

She asked, "What is the job of each post?"

I did not understand the question.

She said, "Every post must have a job. If it has no job, it is noise."

So we wrote the jobs down on paper.

Some posts were trying to impress people.
Some posts were trying to entertain.
Some posts were just showing a product with no meaning.
Some posts were emotional, but had no direction.

Nyakor then gave me a simple system.

"John, you need four kinds of content. Teach. Show. Invite. Sell."

I said, "Sell? People hate selling."

She said, "People hate being pressured. They do not hate being offered something useful."

That was a lesson I needed.

Then she opened her phone and showed me how she scrolls.

She said, "Look. When I see a reel, I am often meeting someone new. When I see a carousel, I am saving something useful. When I watch stories, I am checking if the person is real. When I watch a live, I am deciding whether to trust deeply."

She turned to me and said, "Your problem is not talent. Your problem is that you are using formats randomly. You do not match format to goal."

Then she did the most practical thing.

She told me to choose three pillars.
Plan one week.
Batch my content.
And reuse my best ideas instead of inventing new ones every day.

At first, I resisted.

Because planning felt boring.

But then something happened.

I posted with purpose.
I replied with confidence.
I stopped feeling anxious before posting.

And slowly, engagement became less like weather and more like a result of my actions.

Nyakor was right again.

Guessing feels like freedom.
But systems create power.

What I teach
1) The content mix I use: teach, show, invite, sell

Most creators post too much of one thing.

Some teach too much, and never sell.
Some sell too much, and never build trust.
Some only show pretty photos, and never explain value.
Some invite people to engage, but never guide them to action.

I use a balanced mix.

Not a perfect balance every day.
But a clear mix each week.

Here are the four content jobs.

Teach

Teaching content answers:

- how to do something
- why something matters
- what mistakes to avoid
- what principles guide success

Teaching builds authority.
It builds trust.
It earns saves.

Examples:

- "3 mistakes that kill your reach"
- "How to write a caption that sounds human"
- "How to price your service without fear"

If you sell products, you can still teach:

- care instructions
- how to choose the right option
- the story behind the craft
- how to spot quality

Teaching is not lectures.
Teaching is clarity.

Show

Showing content proves:

- you are real
- your work is real
- your process is honest
- your offer exists in the world

Show is behind the scenes.
Show is proof.
Show is transformation.
Show is the making, the packing, the delivery, the result.

Showing builds credibility fast.

People trust what they can see.

Invite

Inviting content is what creates conversation.

It asks people to participate.
It turns scrolling into engagement.

Invite content includes:

- questions
- polls
- challenges
- prompts
- "choose one" options
- "tell me your situation" posts

This content builds community and increases reach because platforms love interaction.

But the deeper value is human.

People feel seen when you invite them.

Sell

Selling content is where you make an offer.

Not begging.
Not pressure.

A clear offer.

Selling content answers:

- what is available
- who it is for
- what it solves
- what it costs (or how pricing works)
- how to order

Selling content is necessary.

If you never sell, you are building a hobby, not a business.

And remember what Nyakor told me:

People do not hate offers.
People hate feeling used.

If you teach and show and invite with integrity, selling will feel natural, not desperate.

A simple weekly mix that works

Here is a mix I often use:

- Teach: 2 posts
- Show: 2 posts
- Invite: 1 to 2 posts
- Sell: 1 to 2 posts
- Stories: daily light touch
- Live: weekly or biweekly

Adjust based on your business, but keep the mix.

2) Format choices by goal

Formats are not just style.

Formats are strategy.

Different formats do different jobs well.

Reels for reach

Reels are great for discovery.

They help strangers find you.

They work best when:

- the hook is strong
- the visuals are clear
- the message is simple
- the length is tight

Reels are not always best for deep teaching.

They are best for a single idea.

If you want growth, use reels consistently.

But do not rely on reels alone, because reach without trust is weak.

Carousels for saves

Carousels are great for teaching and clarity.

People save them.
People share them.
People return to them.

Carousels work best when:

- the title slide is clear
- each slide is one point
- the design is readable
- the value is practical

Carousels can turn your page into a resource library.

Stories for trust

Stories are the most human format.

They show your daily reality.
They reveal tone.
They build familiarity.

Stories are great for:

- behind the scenes
- quick updates
- polls
- Q and A
- customer reposts
- informal teaching

A page with posts but no stories often feels like a shop that is never open.

Stories keep the lights on.

Lives for depth

Lives build deep trust.

When people hear your voice and see you respond in real time, the relationship becomes stronger.

Lives are great for:

- teaching a topic deeply
- answering questions
- telling your story
- showing a process
- hosting guests or partners

If you want community, lives are powerful.

You do not need long lives.

Even 15 to 25 minutes is enough.

3) Hooks, captions, and calls-to-action that sound human

This is where many people sound fake.

They use copied hooks.
They use dramatic phrases.
They sound like ads.

I want your hooks and captions to sound like a real person talking.

Hooks

A hook is the first line that stops scrolling.

A hook does one of three things:

- promises value
- triggers curiosity
- names a pain

Examples that sound human:

- "If you feel invisible online, read this."
- "I learned this the hard way."
- "Most people post a lot and still don't sell. Here is why."
- "Before you buy, check this."
- "This is the simplest way I plan content weekly."

Avoid hooks that feel like manipulation.

If it sounds like a shouting salesman, people scroll.

Captions

A strong caption has structure.

Not a rigid template that feels robotic.
But a rhythm.

I use a simple flow:

- Hook
- Context
- Value
- Proof or example
- Invite
- Next step

Keep sentences clear.

Do not write like you are applying for a job.
Write like you are speaking to a real person.

Calls-to-action

A call-to-action is what you want people to do next.

Many people say "link in bio" and stop.

But you can be more specific.

Examples:

- "Comment 'PLAN' and I will send you my weekly template."
- "Send me a message with the word 'ORDER' and I will show you options."
- "Save this for later if you want to use it next week."
- "Share this with someone who is building quietly."
- "Which one describes you? A, B, or C?"

The best CTAs match the post.

If the post is educational, ask for a save or share.
If the post is conversational, ask for a comment.
If the post is an offer, ask for a DM or click.

4) Batching and repurposing: one idea, many posts

Consistency is hard when you invent new ideas daily.

The solution is repurposing.

One idea, many posts.

Here is how I do it.

I take one strong topic from my pillar list.

Then I repurpose it into:

- one reel (a quick summary)
- one carousel (a detailed breakdown)
- three story slides (behind the scenes or quick tips)
- one short live (Q and A or deeper teaching)
- one post that sells the related offer

That is one week of content from one idea.

If you do this, you stop feeling pressured.

You stop feeling like content is endless.

You start feeling like content is a system.

Batching also helps if your internet is unstable.

You create content offline.
Then upload when you have signal.

5) Low-budget production that still looks professional

You do not need expensive equipment.

You need clarity and consistency.

Here is what makes content look professional even on a small budget:

Lighting
Natural light near a window is enough.
Avoid dark, grainy visuals.

Audio
If you do voice, make sure it is clear.
Quiet space beats fancy microphone.

Framing
Keep the subject centered.
Do not clutter the background.

Consistency
Use the same colors, style, and tone repeatedly.
Consistency creates brand memory.

Simplicity
One idea per post.
One message per video.

I prefer simple, clean content that feels real.

People trust reality more than perfection.

My action steps

Now I want you to build your weekly system.

Do not aim for perfection.

Aim for consistency.

Action step 1: Build a weekly content plan with 3 pillars

Choose three pillars based on your audience needs and your offer.

Example pillars:

- education
- behind the scenes
- proof and testimonials

Or:

- lifestyle and identity
- product education
- offers and ordering

Now build a weekly plan.

Here is a simple structure:

Monday: Teach (pillar 1)
Tuesday: Show (pillar 2)
Wednesday: Invite (pillar 3)
Thursday: Teach (pillar 1)
Friday: Show proof (pillar 2)
Saturday: Sell (offer)
Sunday: Review and story update

Write your own plan:

Pillar 1:
Pillar 2:
Pillar 3:

Weekly schedule:
Monday:
Tuesday:
Wednesday:
Thursday:
Friday:
Saturday:
Sunday:

Action step 2: Create a reusable caption structure for my brand

Use this structure and adjust your wording:

Hook:
Context:
Value:
Proof or example:
Invite:
Next step:

Write one reusable caption template now.
Then save it in your notes.

When you post, you only fill the blanks.

Action step 3: Make a simple post checklist

Before you publish, check these six points.

Hook: Does the first line stop scrolling?
Value: Is there a clear lesson or benefit?
Proof: Did I show evidence, example, or process?
Invite: Did I ask for engagement?
Next step: Did I tell them what to do next?
Brand fit: Does this match my voice and promise?

Copy this checklist and use it every time.

Closing lesson for this chapter

Engaging content is not luck.

It is purpose.

Teach so people learn.
Show so people trust.

Invite so people participate.
Sell so your business survives.

Match your format to your goal.
Use hooks that sound human.
Reuse your best ideas.

When you stop guessing, content stops draining you.

It starts feeding your growth.

Chapter Six: The art of storytelling
Story thread

I did not grow up thinking of myself as a storyteller in business.

I thought stories belonged to elders around the fire, to churches on Sundays, to friends late at night when the world is quiet.

Business, I believed, should be practical.
Show the product.
Give the price.
Deliver the service.
Move on.

Then one day, Nyakor asked me to watch something with her.

Not a marketing course.
Not a tutorial.

A customer.

We were sitting near a place where people pass by, and a woman was carrying a bag. It was not a luxury bag, but she carried it like it was a crown. She kept adjusting it so the logo faced outward.

Nyakor whispered, "You see? She is not carrying a bag. She is carrying a story."

I laughed, but she was serious.

Nyakor said, "People buy something and then they use it to talk about themselves. They use it to say, 'This is who I am. This is where I belong. This is what I value.'"

That day, I went back to my page and looked at my content again. It was full of facts and features.

But it had little meaning.

I was describing the object, not the identity behind it.

Then Nyakor told me to read my comments again, not for praise, but for clues.

One comment stood out.

"This made more sense to me than what I have been hearing everywhere."

That comment was not about a product.
It was about meaning.

Nyakor said, "When people say something like that, they are asking for a story. They want to carry your message in their pocket."

I asked her, "How do I do that without becoming dramatic or fake?"

Nyakor said, "You do not invent stories. You reveal the stories already inside your work."

She explained that storytelling is not about exaggeration. It is about selecting a true moment, connecting it to meaning, and sharing the lesson in a way people can remember.

Then she made it practical.

She said, "Today, you will post one story. Not a long one. A micro-story."

A micro-story.

She told me to use three parts:
moment, meaning, lesson.

So I did it.

I posted a short scene about a customer who hesitated, fearing scams, and how I proved my work with real steps, and how that became a lesson in trust.

The response shocked me.

People replied.
People shared it.
People said, "This is exactly what I needed."
People started telling me their own stories.

That day, I understood something important.

People do not only buy products.

People buy the story they can carry.

And when you give them a story that matches their values, they feel proud to associate with you.

That is when business becomes deeper than transactions.

It becomes identity.

What I teach
1) Micro-stories that fit short posts: moment, meaning, lesson

You do not need a long essay to tell a story.

On social media, the best stories are short, focused, and memorable.

A micro-story is a small slice of life with a clear point.

I use a simple structure:

Moment
What happened?

One scene.
One event.
One detail that makes it real.

Meaning
Why does it matter?
What does it reveal about people, values, or life?

Lesson
What should the reader take away?
What do I want them to remember or do?

Here is a micro-story example structure you can adapt:

Moment:
"Today a customer asked me, 'How do I know you will deliver?'"

Meaning:
"That question is not only about delivery. It is about fear. People have been disappointed too many times."

Lesson:
"So I decided to build trust publicly: I show my process, I show proof, and I keep my promises."

That is storytelling.

No drama.
No exaggeration.
Just truth with meaning.

How I make micro-stories feel real

I include small details.

Details are what make stories believable.

Examples:

- the time of day
- the place
- the exact words someone said
- a small emotion I felt
- a small action I took

You do not need many details.
Just one or two.

The goal is not to write a novel.

The goal is to make the reader feel, "This is real."

Where to find micro-stories

Many people say, "I have no stories."

That is rarely true.

You have stories every day because you are building something.

Here are places micro-stories hide:

- a customer question
- a mistake you corrected
- a fear you overcame
- a decision you made
- a lesson you learned from failure
- a small win that encouraged you
- a behind-the-scenes struggle
- a moment you chose integrity instead of shortcuts

When you start looking, stories appear everywhere.

2) Behind-the-scenes as trust building, not noise

Behind-the-scenes content can either build trust or waste attention.

The difference is intention.

If your behind-the-scenes content is random, it becomes noise.

If your behind-the-scenes content reveals proof, it becomes trust.

I treat behind-the-scenes content like evidence in a courtroom.

It answers silent questions:

Are you real?
Do you actually do the work?
Is your product quality?
Do you care?
Will you deliver?
Can I trust you with my money?

Behind-the-scenes content can show:

- how you make the product
- how you source materials
- how you package and deliver
- how you handle mistakes
- how you respond to customers
- how you maintain standards

Do not show everything.

Show what builds confidence.

A simple filter I use

Before I post behind-the-scenes, I ask:

Does this build trust?
Does this teach something?
Does this prove quality?
Does this show humanity?

If the answer is no, I keep it private.

3) Customer stories and testimonials as community mirrors

Customer stories are not only marketing.

They are mirrors.

When people see someone like them using your product or learning from your lessons, they think:

"If it worked for them, maybe it can work for me."

That is why testimonials are powerful.

But you must do them well.

Most testimonials are too vague.

"Great service!"
"Nice product!"

That helps a little, but it does not sell deeply.

I prefer testimonials that show:

- the customer's problem before
- what they chose
- what changed after
- how they felt

I also prefer to show the customer's own words, not my rewritten version.

Customer stories should feel like humans talking, not like ads.

How customer stories build community

They do more than sell.

They show that your work is part of people's lives.

They create belonging.

When customers see themselves featured, they feel honored.

When others see customers featured, they think, "This is a community, not a store."

And that is how customers turn into advocates.

4) Visual storytelling: consistent look, clear subject, strong emotion

Visuals are a language.

Most people lose attention because their visuals are confusing.

The viewer cannot tell:
What is the focus?
What is happening?
Why should I care?

I use three rules for visual storytelling.

Consistency
Use consistent colors, fonts, and style.
This makes your content recognizable.

You do not need expensive design.
You need repetition.

Clear subject
In every photo or video, make the subject obvious.

If you sell a product, show it clearly.
If you teach, make your face or your hands visible.
If you show process, focus the camera on the action.

Confusion kills attention.

Strong emotion
Emotion does not mean tears.

Emotion means feeling.

Examples:

- pride in workmanship
- relief after solving a problem
- joy of finishing a task
- calm confidence
- laughter
- struggle
- determination

When your content has feeling, people stop and watch.

Because humans are emotional beings, even when they pretend they are not.

5) Series content that keeps people returning

One of the easiest ways to build loyalty is to build a series.

A series trains people to come back.

It creates anticipation.

It creates habit.

It also makes content creation easier because you are not inventing from scratch every day.

A series can be:

- weekly (best for sustainability)

- daily (if you have high capacity)
- monthly (if your schedule is heavy)

The key is consistency and clarity.

If people do not understand what the series is, they will not follow it.

What makes a series work

- a clear name
- a clear promise (what will people get)
- a consistent day or rhythm
- a consistent style (same look)
- participation (invite people to respond)

The example "Stitches of Strength" works because it suggests:

- craft
- resilience
- progress
- story

Your series name should fit your brand and audience.

My action steps

Now we build your storytelling system.

This is not about talent.
This is about practice.

Action step 1: Write 10 short story prompts from my daily work

These prompts help you find stories without forcing creativity.

Write 10 prompts now.

Use categories to help you.

Customer moments

- A customer asked me _____, and it taught me _____.
- A customer almost walked away because _____, so I did _____.
- A customer said _____, and I realized _____.

Work moments

- Today I struggled with _____, but I learned _____.
- I almost took a shortcut, but I chose _____ because _____.
- I fixed a mistake by _____, and it reminded me _____.

Personal discipline moments

- I did not feel like working, but I did _____ anyway because _____.
- I changed one habit: _____. Here is what happened.
- I used to believe _____. Now I believe _____.

Proof moments

- This is how I make sure quality stays high: _____.
- This is what I check before I deliver: _____.

Now write your own 10 prompts as sentences you can fill.

Keep them in your notes.

Every time something happens, fill one prompt and you have a post.

Action step 2: Create one weekly series

Choose one series for the next four weeks.

Name it.
Define the promise.
Choose the day.

Here is a template:

Series name:
Series promise (one sentence):
Day and time:
Format (reel, carousel, story, live):
How people participate:
How I will feature people:

Example:

Series name: Stitches of Strength
Promise: Every week I share one story of craft, resilience, and the meaning behind what we wear.
Day: Friday
Format: carousel + stories
Participation: followers share their own progress using the hashtag
Feature: I repost 5 stories and highlight one person

Now build yours.

The series should connect to your audience needs and your brand story.

Action step 3: Draft 3 customer spotlight templates I can reuse

Customer spotlights are powerful, but they must be easy to create.

Here are three templates.

Template 1: Before and after

- Before: what problem did they have
- Choice: what did they choose from you
- After: what changed
- Quote: their words
- CTA: "If you relate, message me with _____."

Template 2: Identity and meaning

- Who they are (general, not private details)
- Why they chose it (identity, culture, belonging)
- What it means to them
- Quote
- CTA

Template 3: Process and proof

- What they were worried about
- How you made them feel safe (proof steps)
- The result
- Quote
- CTA

Now customize these templates for your business.

Write them in your note app exactly as you want to reuse them.

Closing lesson for this chapter

Stories are not decoration.

Stories are how humans remember.

Facts inform.
Stories move.

When you tell micro-stories, people carry your message.
When you show behind-the-scenes with intention, people trust.

When you spotlight customers, community grows.
When your visuals are clear and consistent, people recognize you.
When you build a series, people return.

In the next part, we will go even deeper into engagement, management, and conversation.

But for now, start with this:

Do not wait for a perfect story.

Take a real moment.
Give it meaning.
Share the lesson.

That is how your brand becomes memorable.

PART THREE: ENGAGING WITH YOUR AUDIENCE

Part One taught you why visibility matters and how community is built.
Part Two taught you how to craft a presence that is clear, rooted, and trustworthy.

Now Part Three is where many creators either rise or disappear.

Because engagement is not just content.

Engagement is the daily work of being present.

Most people think social media management is simply "posting."

It is not.

Posting is one small piece.

Management is what happens before posting, and what happens after.

Management is planning.
Management is scheduling.
Management is replying.
Management is tracking.
Management is follow-through.

If you can do these well, you will not feel like social media is chaotic.
You will feel like it is a system you control.

And when you control the system, you grow with more peace.

Let us begin.

Chapter Seven: Social media management
Story thread

There was a season when I was posting a lot but feeling poor.

Not only poor in money.
Poor in energy.

Every day felt like panic.

I would wake up and think, "What should I post today?"
Then I would scroll, compare myself to others, feel behind, and post something fast.
I would check my phone every few minutes, waiting for likes like a man waiting for a bus that never arrives.

Nyakor watched me do this for weeks. Then she said something that sounded harsh but was true.

"John, you are not managing your social media. Your social media is managing you."

That sentence made me quiet.

Because I knew it was true.

Social media had become a master, not a tool.

So Nyakor asked me a question.

"Do you run your work like a system or like a mood?"

I did not answer quickly.

Because I knew I was running it like a mood.

If I felt confident, I posted.
If I felt tired, I disappeared.

If I felt inspired, I wrote a long caption.
If I felt discouraged, I stayed silent.

Nyakor said, "A brand cannot survive on moods."

Then she told me to bring a notebook.

She drew four boxes:

Create.
Schedule.
Engage.
Review.

She said, "This is your weekly workflow. You will do the same things every week, in the same order, so your brain stops panicking."

I said, "But I do not have time."

Nyakor laughed.

"You do not have time because you waste it guessing. Systems save time."

Then she asked me to measure something.

She told me to check my phone's screen time.

The number embarrassed me.

I was spending hours on social media, but not building anything strong.

Nyakor said, "You are working hard, but not working smart."

That day, we built a calendar that matched my real capacity, not my fantasy capacity.

We planned my posts for the week.
We batched content when I had stable internet.
We prepared captions offline.
We scheduled uploads when the connection was strong.
We created response windows so I did not live inside my DMs.

We also cleaned my highlights and created a simple folder structure for content so I was not searching for photos like a lost man searching for a goat in tall grass.

Within two weeks, I noticed something.

My stress dropped.
My consistency rose.
My engagement improved.

Not because the algorithm loved me more.

Because I became disciplined.

That was the day I stopped posting randomly.

I started managing my social media like a serious business asset.

What I teach
1) Planning a content calendar that matches my real capacity

A content calendar is not a prison.

It is a peace tool.

It removes daily decision fatigue.

But many people fail because they create calendars that are impossible.

They plan like a rich influencer with a team.

Then reality hits.

They miss a day.
They feel ashamed.
They quit.
They restart.
They repeat the cycle.

So I teach a different approach:

Plan based on what you can sustain, not what looks impressive.

Step one: Identify your true capacity

Ask yourself three questions:

How many posts can I create per week without burning out?
How many stories can I realistically post per day?
How much time can I give to replies daily?

Be honest.

If your true capacity is three posts per week, plan three.
If your true capacity is one post per week, plan one and do it well.

Consistency beats intensity.

Step two: Choose your posting days

I prefer fixed days because they create rhythm.

Example:

Monday: teach
Wednesday: show
Friday: sell or spotlight

Simple.

If you choose random days, you will always be negotiating with yourself.

Fixed days reduce negotiation.

Step three: Match content to your pillars

You already built pillars earlier.

Your calendar should rotate those pillars.

This stops you from repeating the same kind of post and neglecting others.

Step four: Build in flexibility

Life happens.

So I always plan one "flex post."

A flex post is a slot that can be used for:

- a trend that fits
- a customer story
- a quick offer
- a behind-the-scenes moment
- a response to a common question

Flex posts keep the calendar from feeling rigid.

A simple weekly calendar example

If you post three times per week:

- Monday: teach
- Wednesday: behind the scenes
- Friday: offer or customer proof

If you post five times per week:

- Monday: teach
- Tuesday: invite
- Wednesday: show
- Thursday: teach
- Friday: sell
- Weekend: stories and community engagement

Your calendar should fit your life, not fight your life.

2) Scheduling posts and preparing content during stable internet windows

This part is especially important when internet is weak or inconsistent.

When the signal is unstable, you cannot depend on last-minute posting.

You need windows.

I call them "stable internet windows."

These are times when:

- you have Wi-Fi
- the signal is strong
- power is stable
- you can upload without frustration

When you find your windows, you batch your upload work there.

What I prepare offline

Even without internet, I can prepare:

- captions in a note app
- carousel text

- story scripts
- a weekly plan
- content outlines
- video clips recorded and saved
- photo edits

Then when the internet is strong, I only upload.

This makes you faster and calmer.

Scheduling tools

Different platforms allow scheduling in different ways.

Even if you do not use a third-party tool, you can still schedule mentally by preparing drafts.

The core principle is:

Create first. Upload later. Engage after.

Do not do everything at once daily.

That is how burnout happens.

3) Daily community management: comments, DMs, story replies

Posting is the invitation.

Community management is the conversation that follows.

Many people post and then disappear.

Then they complain that people do not buy.

But business grows through conversation.

So I treat engagement like customer service.

What I manage daily

Comments
Comments are public trust signals.

When you reply publicly, others see your tone.
They see your speed.
They see your respect.

That shapes reputation.

DMs
DMs are where buying decisions often happen.

If you reply late or unclear, buyers lose confidence.

Story replies
Story replies are private and personal.
They often contain the most honest questions.

If you treat story replies well, you build strong relationships.

Response windows

To avoid being trapped, I set response windows.

Example:

Morning window: 20 to 30 minutes
Evening window: 20 to 30 minutes

That is enough for most businesses.

If your volume is high, increase windows.

But do not reply all day.

If you reply all day, your brain never rests.

A system protects your mind.

What to prioritize

Not all messages are equal.

I prioritize in this order:

- buying intent messages (pricing, ordering, delivery)
- urgent customer service issues
- genuine questions from engaged community members
- general comments
- low effort messages

This protects revenue and trust.

4) Using features properly: stories, live, highlights, collaborations

Most people underuse platform features.

They post and stop.

But features are built to deepen relationships.

Stories

Stories are where you stay present.

Use stories for:

- quick updates
- polls and questions
- behind-the-scenes
- reposting community posts
- reminders about offers

- human moments

Stories keep your brand alive daily even if you post only three times per week.

Live

Lives build depth.

Use lives for:

- weekly teaching
- Q and A
- behind-the-scenes demonstrations
- customer or partner sessions
- addressing common questions

Lives also create real-time trust.

People see you respond without editing.

Highlights

Highlights are your permanent story library.

They protect your best stories from disappearing.

Use highlights to organize:

- start here
- products/services
- proof
- how to order
- FAQs
- behind-the-scenes
- community rituals

A clean highlight structure reduces repeated questions and speeds up buying.

Collaborations

Collabs expand trust.

But only if they fit your brand.

A good collaboration is not only about reach.

It is about alignment.

Work with:

- creators with similar values
- businesses that serve the same audience but do not compete directly
- community leaders who share your message

Collabs can include:

- joint lives
- shared posts
- shoutouts
- giveaways (only if ethical and relevant)
- co-created content

Do not collaborate with people who damage your reputation.

Your brand is your name in public.

Protect it.

5) Team roles when I can afford help

At first, I did everything myself.

That is normal.

But as you grow, you may need support.

I teach simple roles, even if you cannot hire full-time.

You can use part-time help, interns, or project-based support.

Here are key roles.

Creator
Writes captions, plans content, posts, tracks performance.

Photographer/Videographer
Captures clean visuals, short clips, product shots, behind-the-scenes.

Community replies
Helps respond to comments and DMs based on your approved scripts and standards.

Editor/Designer
Edits reels, designs carousels, keeps brand visuals consistent.

How to start small

If you can only afford one support person, start with the role that saves you most time.

For many product businesses, that is photography and video.

For many service businesses, that is community replies.

Whatever you outsource, keep your voice and standards clear.

Never outsource your integrity.

My action steps

Now we turn this chapter into a weekly system you can run.

Action step 1: Create my weekly workflow (create, schedule, engage, review)

This is the backbone.

Write it in your notebook or notes app.

Here is a simple workflow you can copy.

Create day (1 to 2 hours)

- choose topics for the week
- write captions
- record reels
- take photos
- design carousels

Schedule day (30 to 60 minutes)

- upload posts
- schedule if possible
- prepare stories
- organize drafts

Engage daily (20 to 60 minutes total)

- reply to comments
- reply to DMs
- reply to story replies
- leave meaningful comments on other pages in your niche

Review day (30 minutes weekly)

- check basic metrics
- note what worked
- note what did not
- decide one change for next week

Now write your own version:

My create day:
My schedule day:
My daily engagement windows:
My review day:

Action step 2: Set response standards for DMs and comments

Your response standards protect your brand.

They make your tone consistent.
They make your replies faster.

Write your standards now.

Speed
How fast will you respond?

Example:

- within 2 hours during business hours
- within 24 hours maximum

Tone
Choose three tone rules.

Examples:

- respectful
- clear
- never rude
- never sarcastic
- confident but not arrogant

Structure
I recommend a simple response structure for buying questions:

- answer the question
- give one extra helpful detail
- guide to next step

Example DM reply:

"Yes, we deliver within the city. Delivery is usually same day or next day depending on location. Please send your area name and the item you want, and I will confirm total cost."

Create 5 response templates:

- pricing question
- delivery question
- availability question
- complaint or issue
- thank you message

These templates will save you hours.

Action step 3: Build a simple media folder structure for fast posting

Most people waste time searching for photos and videos.

So I build folders.

You can do this on your phone, laptop, or cloud storage.

Here is a simple structure:

Content

- Reels
    - Raw clips
    - Edited
- Photos
    - Products
    - Behind the scenes
    - Customers (with permission)
- Stories
    - Templates
    - Reposts

- Testimonials
- Brand assets
    - Logo
    - Colors
    - Fonts
    - Bio and links
- Captions
    - Teach
    - Show
    - Invite
    - Sell

This structure helps you post quickly and stay consistent.

Closing lesson for this chapter

If you post randomly, you will live in anxiety.

If you manage your social like a system, you will grow with more peace.

Plan based on real capacity.
Batch content during stable internet windows.
Engage daily with response windows.
Use platform features with intention.
Build a team when you can, but protect your voice and standards.

Social media is not only creativity.

It is management.

And management is what turns attention into trust, and trust into results.

Build a simple media folder structure for fast posting

Before we move into Chapter Eight, I want to tighten this one piece again because it quietly changes everything.

A good folder structure is not "organization for perfection."

It is speed.
It is consistency.
It is peace.

When your media is messy, you waste time.
When your media is clean, you post faster, you repurpose easier, and you stay consistent even when your internet is weak.

Here is the simple structure I use and recommend. You can build it on your phone, laptop, Google Drive, Dropbox, or any storage you trust.

The core rule

One home folder.
Clear subfolders.
The same names every time.

If your naming changes weekly, your system collapses.

Folder structure

SOCIAL MEDIA (HOME FOLDER)

01 BRAND ASSETS

- Logo
- Colors
- Fonts
- Bio versions

- Link text and link destinations
- Brand photos (profile picture, cover, banners)
- Reusable story covers (Start here, Proof, How to order, FAQs)

02 CONTENT BY FORMAT

- Reels
    - 01 Raw
    - 02 Edited
    - 03 Posted
- Photos
    - 01 Products
    - 02 Behind the scenes
    - 03 Lifestyle and identity
    - 04 Team and workspace
    - 05 Customers (permission)
- Carousels
    - 01 Editable templates
    - 02 Finished designs
    - 03 Posted
- Stories
    - 01 Templates
    - 02 Weekly series
    - 03 Proof and testimonials
    - 04 Offers
    - 05 Reposts

03 PROOF LIBRARY

- Testimonials (screenshots)
- Reviews (text)
- Video testimonials
- Before and after
- Case studies
- Delivery proof (packaging, receipts, order logs)
- Press mentions (if any)

04 CAPTIONS AND SCRIPTS

- Teach
- Show
- Invite
- Sell
- Reply templates (DMs and comments)
- Weekly series scripts
- Live outlines

05 CAMPAIGNS AND LAUNCHES

- Month name or campaign name
    - Plan
    - Creative assets
    - Captions
    - Offers
    - Results

06 ARCHIVE

- Old content
- Old templates
- Old brand assets

Naming rules

Use simple names that sort correctly.

Date first, then topic, then format.

Examples:

- 2026-02-08_brandstory_reel_raw
- 2026-02-08_brandstory_reel_edited
- 2026-02-08_testimonial_story
- 2026-02-08_offer_carousel

This makes it easy to search and reuse.

Weekly habit

Every week, do a 10-minute cleanup:

- move posted items into "Posted"
- save great comments or reviews into "Proof Library"
- add new caption drafts into "Captions and Scripts"

This small habit prevents chaos.

Now we move forward.

Chapter Eight: The art of conversation
Story thread

I used to treat replies like a burden.

I would post and then hope the post did well without requiring my time.

When DMs came, I sometimes felt annoyed, not because I hated people, but because I felt overwhelmed.

I thought, "I am busy. I cannot talk all day."

Then Nyakor told me something that changed how I see engagement.

"John, replies are not a distraction. Replies are the business."

I wanted to disagree.

But she was right.

Because when someone replies, they are doing something rare on social media.

They are stepping out of silent scrolling and raising their hand.

They are saying:
"I see you."
"I have a question."
"I am curious."
"I am interested."
"I want to trust you, but I need one more reason."

That is not a distraction.

That is the doorway.

Nyakor made me prove it to myself.

She asked me to open my last 50 DMs and classify them.

We created four categories:

- curiosity (they want to know more)
- doubt (they fear being disappointed)
- urgency (they are ready to act)
- relationship (they just want connection)

Then she asked, "Which of these leads to money?"

I pointed at urgency.

She shook her head.

"All of them can, if you respond well. Because trust grows in conversation."

She then showed me something else.

She said, "Look at your replies."

I read my own replies and felt embarrassed.

They were short, dry, sometimes defensive.

I was answering questions like a tired clerk, not like a guide.

Nyakor said, "You are treating people like interruptions. But they are your opportunity."

Then she taught me a new way to reply.

Not with pressure.
Not with performance.

With curiosity and structure.

She said, "Your job is to keep the thread alive."

That sentence became my new rule.

Because when the thread stays alive, the relationship stays alive. And when the relationship stays alive, business becomes natural.

I started replying differently.

Instead of ending conversations quickly, I opened them wisely.

Instead of pushing an offer, I guided a decision.

Instead of arguing with critics, I protected my dignity.

And slowly, my page began to feel like a living place, not a billboard.

What I teach
1) How I ask better questions so people talk back

Conversation starts with good questions.

Most people ask weak questions like:
"What do you think?"
"Any thoughts?"

Those questions are too open, and people scroll past.

Good questions are specific and easy to answer.

I use four types of questions.

A) Choice questions

These are simple and fast.

Examples:

- "Which one fits you: A or B?"
- "Do you prefer delivery or pickup?"
- "Morning routine or night routine?"

Choice questions reduce effort.

B) Experience questions

These invite personal story.

Examples:

- "What is the hardest part of staying consistent for you?"
- "What did you try that did not work?"
- "When did you first realize you needed this?"

These build connection fast.

C) Opinion questions

These invite values and beliefs.

Examples:

- "Do you think quality matters more than price?"
- "What does integrity look like in business?"

- "What does 'professional' mean to you?"

These deepen community.

D) Action questions

These create participation.

Examples:

- "Show me your workspace today."
- "Post your weekly goal."
- "Use our hashtag and share your progress."

Action questions create user-generated content.

A simple rule for better questions

If someone can answer in five seconds, it is a good social media question.

If they need five minutes to think, it may be too heavy for casual scrolling.

2) How I reply in a way that keeps the thread alive

Most people reply to close.

I reply to open, then guide.

I use a simple structure:

- acknowledge
- answer
- ask a follow-up question
- guide the next step

Example: Comment reply

Comment:
"How much is it?"

Bad reply:
"20 dollars."

Better reply:
"It is 20 dollars. Which size are you looking for, and are you in the city or outside?"

Now the thread stays alive.
Now you have context.
Now you can guide.

Example: DM reply

DM:
"Do you deliver?"

Reply:
"Yes, I deliver. What is your location, and what item are you interested in?"

That reply is short but keeps the conversation moving.

Why follow-up questions matter

Follow-up questions do three things:

- they show you care
- they gather buying information
- they move the person toward a decision

Without follow-up questions, your replies become dead ends.

3) Handling criticism, conflict, and trolls without losing my dignity

If you grow online, you will face criticism.

Some criticism is useful.
Some is noise.
Some is poison.

I handle each differently.

Useful criticism

This is when someone is honest and specific.

Example:
"Your delivery was late."
"The quality was not what I expected."

How I respond:

- I thank them
- I apologize if needed
- I ask for details
- I fix the issue
- I follow up privately

Public humility builds trust.

Noise criticism

This is vague negativity.

Example:
"This is bad."
"Not good."

How I respond:

- one calm reply if needed
- or ignore if it adds no value

Do not feed vague negativity.

Trolls

Trolls want attention.

They insult, mock, provoke.

My rule is simple:
I do not debate trolls.

I protect the space.

Actions:

- hide comment
- delete comment
- block user

If the troll could confuse my audience, I write one calm statement:

"We keep this space respectful. If you have a real concern, share it respectfully. Otherwise, I will remove insults."

Then I stop.

Your dignity is part of your brand.

Do not trade it for a thread.

4) Turning DMs into sales without pressuring people

DMs are where many sales happen, especially for small businesses.

But many people ruin DM sales by pushing too hard.

I use "guiding" instead of "pushing."

Here is my DM flow.

Step 1: Understand their need
Ask:

- what are you looking for
- what is the main problem
- what is your budget range (if appropriate)
- when do you need it

Step 2: Recommend one best option
Do not overwhelm them with ten options.

Give one or two.

Step 3: Reduce risk
Offer proof:

- reviews
- photos
- process
- delivery details
- clear pricing

Step 4: Make the next step simple
Ask for:

- name
- location
- quantity
- preferred payment method
- confirm order

Step 5: Close politely
"Would you like me to reserve this for you today?"

That sentence closes without pressure.

The integrity rule in DMs

Never pretend scarcity if it is not real.
Never shame someone for not buying.
Never pressure people with fear.

You want customers who trust you, not customers who regret.

5) Social listening: finding the language my audience already uses

The best marketing words are not invented.

They are discovered.

Your audience already describes their pain and desire in their own language.

Your job is to listen and reuse that language.

Where do I listen?

- comments on my posts
- comments on competitor posts
- reviews in my niche
- DMs and story replies
- questions people ask repeatedly

I keep a note called "Audience language."

When someone says:
"I feel invisible."
"I don't know what to post."
"I'm tired of scammers."
"I want something that shows who I am."

I save those phrases.

Then I use them in captions, hooks, offers, and replies.

When you speak the audience's language, they feel understood.

And when they feel understood, trust rises.

My action steps

Now we make conversation a system, not a mood.

Action step 1: Create a conversation starter list for captions and stories

Write 20 starters.

Use these categories:

Choice:

- "Which one are you: A or B?"
- "Do you prefer X or Y?"

Experience:

- "What is your biggest challenge with _____?"
- "What did you try that failed?"

Opinion:

- "Do you believe _____?"
- "What does _____ mean to you?"

Action:

- "Show me _____ today."
- "Use our hashtag and share _____."

Write your own list and keep it in your notes.

When you do not know what to post, use a starter.

Action step 2: Write 10 ready-to-use reply templates

You need templates for speed and consistency.

Here are the categories you requested:

Thanks

1. "Thank you. I appreciate your support. What part of this helped you most?"

Clarify
2) "Good question. When you say _____, do you mean _____ or _____?"

Help
3) "I can help with that. What is your situation right now, and what outcome do you want?"

Invite
4) "If you want, send me a message with the word _____ and I will share the details."

Close
5) "Would you like me to reserve this for you today?"

Now add five more templates that match your business:

6. Pricing reply:
7. Delivery reply:
8. Availability reply:
9. Complaint handling:
10. Referral request:

Write them in your "Captions and Scripts" folder so you can copy quickly.

Action step 3: Set boundaries and a moderation rule for my page

Your page is your house.

Write boundaries that protect you and your community.

Examples:

Response boundaries

- I reply within _____ hours during business days.
- I do not respond after _____ time at night unless urgent.

Tone boundaries

- No insults.
- No hate.
- No spam.

Moderation rule

- First disrespectful comment: delete or hide.
- Second: block.
  Or:
- Any hate speech: immediate block.

Write your own:

My boundaries:
My moderation rule:

Closing lesson for this chapter

Conversation is not a side task.

Conversation is where trust is built.

When you ask better questions, people talk back.
When you reply to keep the thread alive, engagement grows.
When you handle criticism with calm strength, your reputation rises.
When you guide DMs into sales respectfully, your income grows.
When you listen to audience language, your content becomes sharper.

Your posts open the door.

Your replies welcome people in.

That is the art of conversation.

Chapter Nine: Building brand advocacy
Story thread

When I first started trying to "grow," I thought the answer was simple.

More followers.

I believed that if I could just add numbers, everything would change.

So I tried the common tricks.

I posted more.
I used trending hashtags without meaning.
I begged people to share.
I even considered giveaways, the kind that attract strangers who only want free things.

Then Nyakor asked me a question that made me stop.

"John, do you want attention or do you want loyalty?"

I said, "Both."

She nodded. "Then stop bribing and start building belonging."

That sentence stayed with me.

Because I had seen what bribery does.

It creates short excitement, then silence.
It attracts people who do not care about your work.
It teaches your audience to wait for rewards instead of trusting your value.

I told Nyakor, "But people do not promote you unless you give them something."

She smiled. "People promote what makes them feel proud. People share what makes them feel seen."

Then she showed me something that made it real.

She opened her own phone and scrolled through her chats.

She pointed at a message:

"Thank you for highlighting my post last week. I felt like my work mattered."

She said, "Look at this. I did not pay her. I did not bribe her. I saw her."

Then Nyakor took me to a small community gathering. Not a big event. Just people meeting under shade, talking about life and work.

I watched how people mentioned names with respect.

"Have you met so-and-so? Their work is solid."
"Go to that one. They deliver."
"That person is honest. They won't disappoint you."

Nobody was bribed.

Advocacy was happening because trust was known and repeated.

Nyakor turned to me and said, "That is what you want online."

Repeated public support.

Not one-time shouting.
Not forced sharing.
Not fake hype.

Repeated support.

So I started paying attention to who was already advocating for me.

Not loudly.

Quietly.

People who returned.
People who referred.
People who commented with meaning.
People who defended my work.
People who used my hashtag.

I stopped treating them like followers.

I started treating them like partners.

I appreciated them publicly.
I featured them.
I asked for their input.
I made them feel like they belonged.

And something shifted.

They began promoting my work without being asked.
They posted their purchases.
They tagged me.
They sent friends.
They used my words.

Not because I bribed them.

Because they felt seen.

That was the day advocacy stopped being a marketing trick.

It became a relationship practice.

What I teach
1) What advocacy really is: repeated public support

Advocacy is not a one-time shoutout.

Advocacy is repeated public support that happens over time.

It looks like:

- a customer posting your product more than once
- someone consistently recommending you in comments
- followers tagging you when others ask for options
- someone using your hashtag without you reminding them
- people defending your brand when someone attacks it unfairly

Advocacy is the difference between:
"I bought once" and "I stand with this brand."

This is why it matters.

Ads can buy attention.
Advocacy multiplies trust.

Because when someone the audience trusts says your name, the fear drops.

Fear is what keeps buyers from acting.

Advocacy reduces fear.

The three levels of advocacy

I teach three simple levels.

Level one: private advocacy
They tell friends in private messages.
They refer quietly.

Level two: public advocacy
They comment publicly.
They tag you publicly.
They post publicly.

Level three: identity advocacy
They integrate your message into who they are.
They use your phrases.
They join your movement.
They become a visible part of your community.

Your job is to help people move from level one to level three.

Not by forcing them.

By building trust and belonging.

2) How I turn buyers into ambassadors

Most businesses treat a sale as the end.

I treat a sale as the beginning.

Because the best buyer is not only the buyer who pays.

The best buyer is the buyer who returns and refers.

So I build a buyer journey that makes people want to advocate.

Here are the three tools I use:

Spotlight.
Appreciation.
Belonging.

Spotlight

Spotlight means you feature them.

You repost their story.
You show their review.
You celebrate their progress.
You highlight their use of your product.

Spotlight tells them:
"You are not just money to me. You are a person."

That feeling is rare online.

So it becomes memorable.

Appreciation

Appreciation is not only "thank you."

It is gratitude with detail.

Instead of:
"Thanks for supporting."

I say:
"Thank you for trusting my work. I noticed you chose the [specific item]. That choice fits your style well. I appreciate you."

That sounds human.

People remember it.

Belonging

Belonging means you make customers feel like part of a circle.

Examples:

- a community hashtag they can use
- a monthly challenge
- a customer highlight series

- a name for your community
- a small ritual like "Friday spotlight"

Belonging turns a customer into a member.

And members advocate.

How I avoid making it awkward

I never pressure people to post.

I invite.

"Thank you again. If you're comfortable, you can share a photo and tag me. It helps others trust. If you share, may I repost?"

That sentence is respectful.

It makes advocacy optional, not forced.

3) Community challenges and user-generated content campaigns

UGC campaigns are advocacy engines when done well.

A good campaign has:

- a simple prompt
- a clear hashtag
- a time window
- a reward that matches your brand
- a spotlight system

But here is the key:

The reward does not need to be money.

Rewards can be:

- public recognition
- featuring someone on your page
- a small bonus item
- a discount for repeat buyers
- early access
- a personal note
- a community badge or title

The most powerful reward for many people is being seen.

What makes challenges work

Keep it easy.

If the task is too hard, people will not participate.

Good tasks:

- "Share your progress"
- "Show how you use it"
- "Tell your story in one paragraph"
- "Post a before and after"
- "Show your workspace today"

Also, repeat the campaign monthly or quarterly.

Repetition trains behavior.

4) Partnerships that expand trust

Partnerships are not only about reach.

Partnerships are trust transfers.

If I collaborate with someone respected, some of their trust flows to me.

But partnerships can also damage you if you partner with the wrong people.

So I use an alignment filter.

My partnership alignment filter

I ask:

Do we share values?
Do we serve overlapping audiences?
Does this partnership help the audience, not only us?
Will I feel proud to be associated with them?
Does their reputation protect or endanger mine?

If the answers are good, I proceed.

Types of partnerships that work well

Creators
People who create content and have influence in a niche.

Cultural groups
Communities built around identity, art, language, faith, or shared heritage.

Aligned businesses
Businesses that serve the same audience but do not compete directly.

Examples:
If you sell clothing, partner with photographers, salons, stylists, tailors, cultural dance groups.
If you teach marketing, partner with web designers, copywriters, small business associations.

Partnership formats

- joint live sessions
- shared posts
- a co-hosted challenge
- guest features

- bundle offers (if ethical)
- community events

Remember:
The goal is not to borrow attention.
The goal is to expand trust.

5) Building a movement with a hashtag

A movement is bigger than a campaign.

A movement is a shared identity people want to be part of.

And a hashtag can become the rally point for that movement.

But only if it stands for something real.

A movement hashtag is not:
"Buy my product."

A movement hashtag is:
"This is what we believe."
"This is how we live."
"This is the kind of work we respect."
"This is the kind of life we are building."

When your hashtag becomes a shared identity, people use it proudly.

They feel like they are part of a bigger story.

This is the deepest form of advocacy.

Because now they are not promoting you only as a seller.

They are promoting a message that reflects them.

The discipline required

Movements require consistency.

You must:

- use the hashtag regularly
- feature people who use it
- tell stories tied to it
- protect the community tone
- keep the meaning clear

A dead hashtag is a sign of a dead ritual.

So you must keep it alive with structure.

My action steps

Now we turn advocacy into a repeatable system.

Action step 1: Design a monthly advocacy campaign (prompt, hashtag, reward, spotlight)

Use this simple blueprint:

Prompt
What do you want people to share?

Examples:

- "Share how you use it"
- "Share your weekly progress"
- "Share your story in one paragraph"
- "Share a before and after"

Hashtag
Create or reuse your community hashtag.

Keep it short and clear.

Reward
Choose a reward that fits your brand.

Examples:

- feature on your page
- small discount for repeat buyers
- free delivery for one winner
- bonus item
- early access
- a personal thank you note

Spotlight
Decide how you will feature participants.

Examples:

- repost 5 stories per week
- highlight 1 person weekly
- create a monthly collage carousel of participants
- go live and shout out contributors

Now write your campaign:

Campaign name:
Prompt:
Hashtag:
Time window (example: 1st to 7th monthly):
Reward:
Spotlight plan:
How people enter:
How you choose winners (if any):
How you announce results:

If you repeat this monthly, you will train advocacy.

Action step 2: Create a referral and repeat-buyer message that feels personal

You need a message you can send after a successful delivery or service.

Here are two templates you can customize.

Referral message template
"Thank you again for trusting my work. If you know someone who would benefit from this, you can share my page or tag me when they ask. I will take care of them the same way. I appreciate you."

Repeat-buyer message template
"I enjoyed serving you. If you ever want another one or a different option, just message me and I'll show you what's available. I also keep a small list of returning customers so I can notify them when something new drops. Would you like me to add you?"

These messages are warm and respectful, not pushy.

Customize them for your business and save them as templates.

Action step 3: Draft a collaboration outreach script

Partnership outreach should feel human, not like spam.

Keep it short, respectful, and clear.

Here is the script structure I use:

- greet them by name
- mention something specific you respect about their work
- explain the shared value for the audience
- propose one simple collaboration format
- make it easy to say yes or no

Template:

"Hi [Name]. I've been following your work, especially [specific detail]. I serve [your audience], and I think our audiences overlap in a helpful way. Would you be open to a simple collaboration, like a short live session or a shared post on [topic]? I believe it would help people [benefit]. If you're interested, I can suggest two time options and a simple outline."

Now customize it:

Your outreach script:

Also create two variations:

- one for creators
- one for businesses
- one for cultural groups

Keep them in your "Reply templates" folder.

Closing lesson for this chapter

Advocacy is earned.

It is earned through repeated trust, not bribery.

When people feel seen, they speak.
When they feel respected, they return.
When they feel belonging, they promote.

Build spotlight systems.
Build appreciation habits.
Build community challenges.
Build partnerships that expand trust.
Build a movement with a meaningful hashtag.

If you do this, your followers will not just watch.

They will carry your name with pride.

PART FOUR: MEASURING SUCCESS AND GROWTH

Growth feels good, but feelings can lie.

One week you feel like you are winning because likes are high, yet sales are flat.
Another week you feel like you are failing because reach is down, yet inquiries are rising.

This is why measuring matters.

When I measure, I stop guessing. I stop arguing with my mood. I stop blaming the algorithm for everything. I start seeing what is actually happening.

And once I can see it, I can improve it.

Chapter Ten: Tracking your results
Story thread

I used to fight with social media like a man arguing with smoke.

If a post did well, I assumed I had cracked the secret.
If a post did badly, I assumed the platform hated me.

My confidence rose and fell with numbers I did not understand.

One day Nyakor watched me complain after a post got low engagement.

I said, "This platform is unfair. People are not seeing my work."

Nyakor did not disagree. She asked one question.

"What is your proof?"

I said, "Look at the likes. Look at the reach."

She said, "Those are feelings in number form. They do not tell the full story."

Then she opened my insights and started scrolling like someone reading a report, not like someone seeking comfort.

She said, "John, you are arguing with your emotions. You are not using evidence."

That sentence hit me hard because it was true.

Nyakor pointed at one post with low likes and asked, "How many saves?"

The saves were high.

She said, "This is not a bad post. This is a valuable post."

Then she pointed at another post with high likes and asked, "How many profile visits? How many link clicks? How many inquiries?"

The answer was low.

She said, "This one made people smile. It did not move them."

I stared at the numbers and felt embarrassed.

I had been measuring my business like a child measures success in applause.

Nyakor said, "Your goal is not applause. Your goal is outcomes."

Then she asked me to define my goal for the next 30 days.

I said, "More followers."

She said, "Why?"

I paused.

Nyakor smiled. "Followers are not the goal. Followers can help the goal. What do you want followers to do?"

That was the moment everything became clear.

We sat down and wrote it plainly:

Awareness.
Leads.
Sales.
Repeat buyers.
Referrals.

Then she said, "Now you will track like a business owner, not like a performer."

She taught me how to choose metrics that match the goal, how to track inquiries and website traffic, how to log weekly numbers without fancy tools, and how to read patterns without panic.

Most importantly, she taught me to be honest about attribution.

She said, "Social media often influences the sale before it closes. Do not lie to yourself. Learn the difference."

That day, analytics stopped being a scary word.

It became a mirror.

And mirrors, when used well, do not insult you.

They teach you.

What I teach
1) The metrics that matter by goal

Most people track what is easiest to see, not what matters.

Likes are easy.
Followers are easy.

But business outcomes are deeper.

So I start with the goal, then I choose the metrics that prove progress toward that goal.

Goal: Reach and awareness

This is the stage where strangers discover you.

Metrics that matter:

- Reach (unique accounts reached)
- Impressions (total views)
- Video views (especially for reels and short videos)
- Follows gained from content (not total followers only)
- Profile visits

What it tells me:

- Are new people discovering me?
- Are my hooks and visuals stopping the scroll?
- Is my content getting distributed beyond my current followers?

A warning sign:
High impressions with low profile visits usually means the content entertained but did not create curiosity.

Goal: Trust and engagement

This is where people start to care.

Metrics that matter:

- Saves (people want to return)
- Shares (people want others to see it)
- Comments (public conversation)
- Story replies (private trust)
- DM volume (especially questions, not just greetings)
- Average watch time (for videos)

What it tells me:

- Do people value this enough to keep it?
- Are they willing to attach their name to it by sharing?
- Are they comfortable enough to speak back?

A warning sign:
High likes with low saves and shares often means shallow engagement.

Goal: Leads and inquiries

This is where interest becomes action.

Metrics that matter:

- Link clicks
- Website visits from social (if you have it)
- WhatsApp clicks (if you use WhatsApp)
- DMs that include buying intent (price, availability, delivery, booking)
- Form fills (if you use forms)
- Calls booked (if you sell services)

What it tells me:

- Did my content create enough confidence for someone to move?
- Is my call to action clear?
- Is my profile setup doing its job?

A warning sign:
High profile visits but low inquiries often means your bio, highlights, pinned posts, or offer clarity needs work.

Goal: Sales

This is where money changes hands.

Metrics that matter:

- Orders (count)
- Revenue (amount)
- Conversion rate (leads to sales)
- Average order value (if you sell products)
- Close rate from DMs (if you sell through chat)

What it tells me:

- Is my audience buying?
- Is my offer priced well for the market?
- Are my replies and follow-through strong?

A warning sign:
Lots of inquiries but few sales can point to pricing mismatch, weak proof, slow replies, or unclear ordering process.

Goal: Repeat buyers and referrals

This is where your business becomes stable.

Metrics that matter:

- Repeat purchase count
- Referral count

- Customer-generated posts tagging you
- Use of your community hashtag by customers
- Testimonials collected

What it tells me:

- Do people trust me enough to return?
- Do they trust me enough to risk their reputation by referring others?

A warning sign:
Sales happen but repeat buyers are low. That often means the experience is not strong enough, the delivery is inconsistent, or the relationship ends after the sale.

2) How I track what social contributes to website traffic and inquiries

Many people say, "Social is not working," because they only measure sales.

But social often works like a bridge.

People see your content today.
They think about it.
They watch again tomorrow.
They ask a friend.
They return next week.
Then they buy.

If you only track immediate purchases, you will miss the influence.

So I track contribution in simple ways.

Tracking inquiries from social

I do two things:

First, I tag conversations.
If I use WhatsApp or DMs, I create a simple habit:
Whenever someone asks about buying, I note the source.

Examples:

- IG story reply
- IG reel
- Facebook post
- TikTok video
- Referral from customer
- Website contact form

Second, I ask one question gently:
"How did you find me?"

This is not interrogation. It is curiosity.

Over time, the answers reveal the truth.

Tracking website traffic from social

If I have a website, I track:

- clicks from social to the website
- which pages they visit (if I can see that)
- which campaigns drive visits

If I do not have analytics set up, I still track clicks using basic link tracking, which I will teach below.

The point is simple:
If people are clicking, your content is moving them.
If they are not clicking, your content may be visible but not persuasive.

3) Simple tracking without fancy tools

You do not need complex dashboards.

You need consistency.

I use two levels of tracking:

- a weekly log
- a monthly review

Weekly log

Once per week, on the same day, I record five numbers.

Not twenty.

Five.

Why five?
Because simplicity keeps me consistent.

The weekly log answers:
Is my system working?
Is it improving?
What changed?

I keep the log in a notebook, a note app, or a spreadsheet.

The format is simple:
Week of (date)
Metric 1:
Metric 2:
Metric 3:
Metric 4:
Metric 5:
Notes (one paragraph)

Monthly review

Once per month, I do a deeper review.

I do not only look at totals. I look for patterns.

I ask:

- What increased and why?
- What dropped and why?
- Which content drove the most saves?
- Which content drove the most DMs?
- Which content drove the most clicks?
- Which offer performed best?
- What should I repeat next month?
- What should I stop?

No shame.
No drama.
Just learning.

4) How I read patterns

Nyakor taught me a simple truth:

One post is a moment.
Patterns are a message.

So I do not change my strategy because of one bad day.

I look for repeated signals across weeks.

Here are the patterns I watch closely.

What people save

Saves often mean:

- this is useful
- this is worth returning to
- this feels like a guide

When saves are high, I ask:
What topic was it?

What format was it?
Was it a clear checklist, a process, or a lesson?

Then I create more content in that family.

What people share

Shares often mean:

- this is identity
- this is strong enough to attach my name to it
- this will help my friend

When shares are high, I ask:
Was it emotionally strong?
Was it culturally meaningful?
Was it a clear truth people wanted to repeat?

Then I create more content that hits the same nerve.

What people ignore

Low reach or low engagement can mean several things:

- weak hook
- unclear subject
- too long
- too complex
- wrong timing
- not aligned with audience needs

I do not call it failure.

I call it feedback.

I ask:
What was the job of the post?
Did it do that job?

Sometimes the post "fails" because I gave it the wrong job.

Example:
I posted a deep teaching point as a reel when it should have been a carousel.
The content was good. The format was wrong.

5) Attribution honesty: "influenced by social" versus "closed by social"

This is where many marketers lie to themselves.

They want a clean story:
"This post caused this sale."

But reality is messy.

Social media often does two things:

- it influences
- it assists the close

Sometimes it closes directly, especially when someone DMs after a story and buys.

But many times, social influence is the reason someone trusts you enough to buy through another channel later.

So I track two categories.

Influenced by social

This means:
They saw me on social, built trust, then bought later.

Examples:

- they saw my reels for weeks, then visited my shop

- they watched stories, then asked a friend, then bought
- they followed, then later came through referral

Closed by social

This means:
The sale happened directly through social action.

Examples:

- they DM and pay
- they click the link and purchase
- they book a call from my profile link

Both matter.

If I only count "closed by social," I may undervalue social.
If I pretend everything is "closed by social," I fool myself.

Honesty protects strategy.

My action steps
Action step 1: Set my weekly scorecard (5 numbers only)

Choose five numbers based on your current goal.

Here are three ready-made scorecards depending on what you are building.

If your goal is awareness:

- Reach
- Profile visits
- Follows gained
- Shares
- Saves

If your goal is leads:

- Profile visits
- Link clicks (or WhatsApp clicks)
- DMs with buying intent
- Story replies
- Leads captured (form fills or call bookings)

If your goal is sales and repeat buyers:

- Inquiries (buying intent DMs)
- Sales (orders or revenue)
- Close rate (sales divided by inquiries)
- Repeat buyers
- Referrals or testimonials collected

Pick one set and stick to it for 4 weeks before changing.

That is how you see patterns.

Action step 2: Create a monthly review page: wins, losses, lessons, next tests

Create one page for each month.

Use this structure:

Month:
Primary goal:

Wins:

- What worked? (3 to 5 bullets)
- Which post performed best and why?
- Which offer performed best and why?

Losses:

- What did not work? (3 to 5 bullets)
- Where did I waste time?
- What content failed and what likely caused it?

Lessons:

- What did I learn about my audience?
- What language did they use repeatedly?
- What objections kept showing up?

Next tests:

- One thing I will stop
- One thing I will start
- One thing I will improve
- One simple experiment (test one variable only)

Write it like a coach talking to yourself, not like a judge sentencing yourself.

Action step 3: Add a basic link tracking method for campaigns

You do not need fancy tools to track links.

Here are three simple methods, from easiest to stronger.

Method A: Unique keyword in DMs
For each campaign, choose one keyword and tell people to message you with it.

Examples:

- "Message me with ORDER"
- "Message me with PLAN"
- "Message me with GUIDE"

Then count how many messages you get with that keyword.

This is simple and powerful.

Method B: Separate links per campaign
If you have one main link in bio, create separate links for:

- product offer
- booking
- free guide
- campaign page

Then rotate the link during the campaign and track clicks using the platform's link click metric.

Method C: UTM-style naming, even if you do it manually
If you can add a small label to your link destination, do it.

Example idea:
Create separate landing pages or separate forms for each campaign:

- /offer-feb
- /offer-march
- /guide-reels

Then you can clearly see which campaign drove which action.

The goal is not perfection.
The goal is clarity.

Closing lesson for this chapter

Analytics is not there to shame you.

Analytics is there to free you from feelings.

When I track, I stop guessing.
When I track, I learn faster.
When I track, I improve with purpose.

Choose metrics that match your goal.
Track contribution, not only direct sales.
Keep it simple weekly, deeper monthly.
Read patterns, not single posts.
Be honest about influence versus close.

And remember this:

If you do not measure, you cannot improve.
If you measure well, growth becomes repeatable.

Chapter Eleven: Adapting and updating
Story thread

There was a time when I thought consistency meant never changing.

I believed that if I adjusted my content, it meant I was unstable.
If I updated my offers, it meant I had failed.
If I tried a new format, it meant I had been doing it wrong all along.

So I held onto old habits like a man holding onto a worn-out shoe because it once carried him far.

But growth has a way of forcing honesty.

As my audience grew, pressure grew with it.

People asked for new things.
They wanted faster replies.
They wanted different price options.
They wanted more content.
They wanted me to "do what everyone is doing."

And inside me, another pressure rose.

Fear.

Fear that if I change, I will lose my identity.
Fear that if I adapt, I will look like a copycat.
Fear that if I try something new, I will fail in public.

Nyakor saw the war inside me.

One evening she said, "John, you are confusing two things."

"Identity is who you are. Strategy is how you serve. Strategy can change without you becoming someone else."

That sentence made me breathe.

Because it gave me permission.

It told me I could update my approach without betraying my values.

But Nyakor also warned me.

She said, "If you adapt without discipline, you will chase trends and lose yourself. If you refuse to adapt, you will become outdated and invisible."

So she taught me how to adapt safely.

She taught me how to test one change at a time.
How to separate trend from truth.
How to refresh my plan based on real feedback, not noise.
How to expand formats without burning out.
How to keep quality high when growth brings pressure.

And as I practiced, I learned something powerful:

Updating is not weakness.

Updating is stewardship.

When you update, you protect what you are building from becoming stale.
When you update with integrity, you stay alive without becoming fake.

That is the balance.

What I teach
1) How I test changes safely: one change at a time

Most creators change everything at once.

They change their style, their format, their captions, their posting time, their offers, their tone, their niche, their hashtags, and then they say:

"Nothing works."

Of course nothing works.

They have no idea what caused what.

Nyakor taught me the simplest testing rule:

One change at a time.

If you change one thing, you can learn.
If you change ten things, you create confusion.

This rule protects your mind and your business.

What counts as "one change"

One change can be:

- switching from carousels to reels for one pillar
- changing posting time for two weeks
- adjusting the first line of your captions
- adding one clear call to action
- adding a new offer format (bundle, mini-package)
- changing your content mix (teach/show/invite/sell ratio)

One change does not mean changing your identity.

You keep your voice.
You keep your values.
You test one lever.

Testing time frame

A test must run long enough to show a pattern.

I recommend:

- at least 2 weeks for small tests (posting time, hook style)
- 4 weeks for bigger tests (content mix, new format series)
- one full cycle for offers (launch, follow-up, close)

If you test for two days, you are not testing.

You are reacting.

What I write down before the test

Before I test, I write:

- what I am changing
- why I am changing it
- what metric will show success
- what I will keep the same

Example:

Change: post reels at 7 PM instead of 9 AM
Why: my audience replies more in evenings
Metric: reach + DMs with buying intent
Keep the same: topic, style, call to action

Now I can learn.

2) When to follow a trend and when to ignore it

Trends are not evil.

But trends are not truth.

A trend is simply a wave.

If you ride every wave, you will never reach your destination.

I follow trends only when they meet my filter.

My trend filter

I ask five questions:

Does this trend fit my brand voice?
Does it match my audience needs?
Can I adapt it without looking fake?
Will it help my goal (reach, leads, sales)?
Can I do it with quality, not rush?

If the answer is yes, I use the trend.

If the answer is no, I ignore it.

Because attention gained through fake behavior is expensive.

It costs trust.

Trend discipline: the 80/20 rule

Even when I use trends, I keep them small.

About 80 percent of my content stays evergreen:

- lessons
- proof
- stories
- offers
- community rituals

About 20 percent can be trend-based.

This protects identity.

Evergreen content builds stability.
Trend content can boost reach.

But evergreen is what builds trust.

3) Refreshing my content plan based on feedback and results

Updating should not be random.

Updating should be informed.

Nyakor taught me to refresh my plan using three sources:

- analytics patterns
- audience feedback
- business needs

Analytics patterns

What is performing well?

- high saves
- high shares
- high DMs
- high link clicks
- strong watch time

Those are signals.

I do more of what performs.

What performs poorly consistently?

Those are also signals.

But I do not kill content just because it did not go viral.

I ask:
Did it do its job?

Some posts are not meant to get massive reach.
Some posts are meant to close buyers.

So I judge content by goal.

Audience feedback

Feedback comes in:

- comments
- DMs
- story replies
- poll responses
- the questions people ask repeatedly

If people keep asking the same question, that question should become content.

If people misunderstand your offer, you need clearer proof content.

If people ask for different options, you may need to update your packages or pricing tiers.

Business needs

Sometimes you update because business reality changes.

Example:

- you added a new service
- you changed delivery areas
- your costs increased
- demand increased and you need to limit custom orders
- you want to focus on a higher-margin offer

Your content plan must serve your business, not only your creativity.

4) Expanding to new formats without burning out

A common mistake is trying to master everything at once.

People say:
"I must do reels, carousels, stories, lives, long videos, newsletters, podcasts, and blog posts."

Then they burn out.

I expand formats slowly.

The one-format expansion rule

I add one new format at a time.

For example:

Month 1: stories daily + 3 posts weekly
Month 2: add one live weekly
Month 3: add one reel weekly
Month 4: add a carousel series

Slow growth is sustainable growth.

Reuse is the secret

When I add a new format, I do not create new ideas.

I repurpose.

One idea becomes:

- a reel
- a carousel

- a story sequence
- a live outline

So adding formats does not double effort.

It multiplies reach from the same content.

Protecting energy

I protect energy by setting boundaries:

- batch content once per week
- reply in windows, not all day
- reuse templates
- keep series content consistent
- stop chasing daily perfection

A tired creator becomes inconsistent.

Inconsistent presence kills momentum.

So energy is not optional.

Energy is strategy.

5) Keeping quality high when growth creates pressure

Growth is good, but growth creates pressure.

More messages.
More demands.
More expectations.
More noise.

If you are not careful, you will reduce quality to keep up.

And when quality drops, trust drops.

Nyakor taught me to protect quality with systems.

Quality protection systems

Standard operating steps
A checklist for:

- posting
- customer service
- delivery or fulfillment
- content review

Templates

- captions
- reply scripts
- offers
- onboarding messages

Limits

- limit custom work if it overwhelms you
- limit daily DM time
- limit how many offers you run at once

Clear communication

- realistic delivery times
- clear pricing
- clear ordering steps

The goal is to stay reliable.

A brand becomes respected when people can predict you in a good way.

Predictability in integrity is a gift.

My action steps
Action step 1: Choose 2 experiments for next month

Pick two experiments only.

One should be a format test.
One should be a timing or workflow test.

Here are examples.

Format tests

- Test one reel per week for one pillar
- Turn one teaching post into a carousel each week
- Test a weekly live Q and A
- Test a "series" format (same day, same name)

Posting time tests

- Post at two different time windows and compare results
- Shift stories to morning and evening windows
- Schedule posts during your stable internet window and measure consistency

Now write your two experiments:

Experiment 1 (format):
What I will change:
Why:
Metric:
Duration:
What stays the same:

Experiment 2 (timing/workflow):
What I will change:
Why:
Metric:

Duration:
What stays the same:

Action step 2: Rewrite 3 underperforming posts using what I learned

Underperforming posts are not trash.

They are raw material.

Often the idea is good, but the delivery was weak.

Choose three posts that:

- had low reach
- or low saves
- or low DMs
- or low clarity

Then rewrite them using these improvement moves:

Stronger hook

- speak to a real pain or desire
- make the first line clear and specific

Clearer value

- one idea
- one takeaway
- one action

Better proof

- add an example
- add a screenshot
- add behind-the-scenes
- add a short story

Stronger invitation

- ask a specific question
- tell them what to do next

Now list your three posts:

Post 1:
What went wrong:
Rewrite plan:

Post 2:
What went wrong:
Rewrite plan:

Post 3:
What went wrong:
Rewrite plan:

Then repost them across new formats:

- turn one into a reel
- turn one into a carousel
- turn one into a story sequence

This is how you upgrade without inventing new content.

Action step 3: Create a "stop doing" list to protect my energy

This is one of the most powerful actions in the whole book.

Growth is not only about what you start doing.

Growth is also about what you stop doing.

Write your stop list now.

Examples:

Stop doing:

- posting without a goal
- rewriting captions forever
- scrolling competitors until I feel small
- replying instantly all day
- taking every custom request
- joining every trend
- arguing with trolls
- creating content without proof

Now create your own stop doing list.

Keep it visible.

Because every "stop" is energy returned to you.

And energy is what fuels consistency.

Closing lesson for this chapter

Adapting does not mean abandoning yourself.

Adapting means serving better.

Test one change at a time so you can learn.
Follow trends only when they fit your brand and goal.
Refresh your plan based on evidence and feedback.
Expand formats slowly, repurposing instead of doubling work.
Protect quality with systems, limits, and clear communication.

If you master updating, you will not fear change.

You will use change as a tool.

And you will grow without losing who you are.

Chapter Twelve: Beyond the basics
Story thread

There is a moment in business when you realize something that is both exciting and dangerous.

Your work is no longer only local.

People you have never met start finding you.
People from other cities begin asking for delivery.
People from other countries begin asking questions.
Someone tags you in a group you did not know existed.
A creator reposts your content and suddenly your notifications feel like rain on a tin roof.

At first, I enjoyed it.

It felt like victory.

Then reality showed its face.

The questions multiplied.
The expectations multiplied.
The pressure multiplied.

And the risk multiplied too.

Because global attention can lift a brand, but it can also expose weakness fast.

If your ordering process is messy, attention becomes chaos.
If your customer support is slow, attention becomes complaints.
If your brand voice is unclear, attention becomes misunderstanding.
If you are culturally careless, attention becomes offense.

Nyakor warned me early.

She said, "John, local growth forgives mistakes. Global growth punishes them."

That sentence made me serious.

Because I had seen it happen.

A small brand can survive a few mistakes because customers know the person behind it.
A global audience does not know you.

They judge you only by what they see.

Nyakor then told me the truth about the next level.

"Beyond the basics is not about being famous. It is about being prepared."

Prepared to collaborate without becoming fake.
Prepared to use paid promotion without wasting money.
Prepared to turn attention into a real business system.
Prepared to respect other cultures while staying rooted.
Prepared to handle opportunities like a professional, not like a desperate person.

That was the day I stopped thinking of growth as only numbers.

I started thinking of growth as responsibility.

Because the bigger your reach, the bigger your duty to be clear, honest, and consistent.

Now in this chapter, I will teach you how I approach growth with maturity.

What I teach
1) Creator partnerships and influencer campaigns that do not feel fake

Influencers can help a brand grow fast.

But influencer marketing also has a reputation problem.

Many campaigns look fake.
Many creators promote products they do not use.
Many brands chase fame instead of fit.
And audiences are not stupid.

They can smell dishonesty.

So I treat creator partnerships like trust deals.

If trust is damaged, the campaign is expensive even if it "works."

The two kinds of creator partnerships

I use two categories.

Community creators
These are creators with smaller audiences but strong trust.
Their followers listen because the relationship is close.

This is often the best place to start.

Big creators
These are larger influencers with big reach.
They can create rapid awareness, but they can also be costly and less personal.

Both can work.

But in early growth, community creators often give a better return because trust is deeper.

My creator partnership standards

I follow these standards to avoid fake campaigns:

Alignment first
The creator must fit the brand values and audience.

Proof of real use
If possible, the creator should use the product or experience the service before promoting it.

Creative freedom within brand rules
I give them talking points, not scripts.
Scripts create robotic content.

Clear deliverables
What are they posting?
When?
Which platforms?
How many pieces of content?
Will they tag and link?

Clear disclosure
If it is sponsored, it must be disclosed.
This is not only ethics. It protects brand credibility.

The "story-based campaign" approach

The best influencer promotions do not feel like ads.

They feel like stories.

Instead of:
"Buy this now."

The creator shares:

- why they tried it
- what problem it solved

- what surprised them
- how it fit their life
- who it is best for

That is real.

That is why I prefer campaigns built around:

- unboxing stories
- before and after
- first-time experience
- "a week using this"
- "my honest review"

When the creator tells a story, the audience trusts more.

2) Paid promotion basics for small budgets

Paid promotion is powerful, but it can also waste money fast.

Small businesses often make two mistakes:

They boost everything.
Or they boost the wrong thing.

Nyakor taught me a simple rule:

Boost the right post, not every post.

Paid promotion works best when you already have proof that the content performs organically.

If a post is already getting good reach, saves, shares, or comments, it is a better candidate for boosting.

If a post is dead organically, boosting usually amplifies dead content.

What to boost

I boost content that does one of these jobs:

Top-of-funnel awareness
A clear reel or short video that introduces the brand and performs well.

Lead generation
A post that leads people to a link or DM with a keyword.

Offer post
A clear offer post that already brings inquiries.

Proof post
Testimonials and strong social proof that builds trust.

Small budget strategy

If your budget is small, do not spread it thin.

Use short focused campaigns.

Example:

- boost one strong post for 5 to 7 days
- monitor results
- adjust
- repeat

Targeting basics

Even without deep technical skill, I focus on:

- location (if local delivery matters)
- interests (aligned with niche)
- age range (if relevant)
- language (if you market in a specific language)

But I keep it simple.

Complicated targeting can confuse small campaigns.

The key lesson about paid promotion

Paid promotion does not fix a weak offer.

If your profile is confusing, ads will send people to confusion.
If your ordering process is unclear, ads will create frustration.

So paid promotion must come after basic clarity is built.

3) Turning attention into a real business

Attention is not success.

Attention is raw material.

Success is what you do with attention.

This is where many creators fail.

They go viral, then they waste it.

They have no clear offer.
No clear ordering process.
No customer support system.
No follow-up.

So the attention disappears like water poured on sand.

Nyakor taught me to treat attention like a visitor entering a shop.

When someone enters, they need:

- direction
- clarity

- proof
- an easy next step

Offers

At the beyond-basic level, your offers must be clear.

One main offer is better than ten unclear offers.

You can have variety, but your core offer should be easy to understand.

Ask:
What do I sell?
Who is it for?
What does it solve?
What is the price range?
How do you order?

Ordering process

If you sell through DMs, create a consistent ordering script.

Example:

- greet
- confirm item
- confirm price
- confirm delivery location
- confirm time
- confirm payment
- send receipt or confirmation

If you sell through a website, create a simple checkout.

Do not make people fight for the purchase.

Customer support

As you grow, support becomes the brand.

People will forgive small delays if your communication is clear. They will not forgive silence.

So I build support rules:

- response windows
- templates
- escalation steps
- refund or replacement policy (if needed)
- clear delivery timelines

Support is not only fixing problems.

Support is preventing problems.

4) Cultural sensitivity when selling globally

This is one of the most underestimated parts of global growth.

When you sell locally, your culture is assumed.
People understand your humor.
They understand your tone.
They understand your references.

When you sell globally, misunderstandings multiply.

Cultural sensitivity does not mean you hide who you are.

It means you respect who others are.

It protects your brand from accidental offense and unnecessary conflict.

Where cultural sensitivity matters most

Language
Words that sound normal in one place can sound rude in another.

Imagery
Colors, symbols, and gestures can carry different meanings.

Religion and identity
Some phrases can be sensitive.

Gender norms and family norms
Marketing messages can land differently.

Pricing and negotiation expectations
Some markets expect fixed prices, others expect negotiation.

Customer service expectations
Some cultures expect very fast responses, others expect formal greetings.

My cultural sensitivity practices

I do these things:

- I avoid insulting humor
- I avoid stereotypes
- I avoid making political jokes
- I ask questions when I am unsure
- I focus on universal values: dignity, quality, honesty, service
- I explain my policies clearly to avoid confusion

Cultural sensitivity is not weakness.

It is maturity.

And it protects your brand reputation long-term.

5) Preparing for big opportunities

Big opportunities can come suddenly:

- a media request
- an event invitation
- a partnership offer
- a distributor inquiry
- a viral moment
- a feature by a large page

If you are not prepared, you will waste the opportunity.

Nyakor told me, "You must be press ready before the press arrives."

That means having:

- clear brand story
- clean visuals
- professional contact method
- quick response process
- product photos ready
- pricing and ordering clarity
- a short pitch you can repeat

Media requests

If someone asks for an interview or story, be ready with:

- a short bio
- your origin story
- why your work matters
- clear examples of impact
- high-quality photos

Events

If you attend events, be ready with:

- a one-minute introduction
- a simple brochure or digital flyer
- QR code to your link or page
- a clear offer for event attendees
- a follow-up plan

Growth planning

When growth comes, ask:
What will break first?

Usually it is:

- delivery capacity
- customer support time
- inventory
- quality control

So plan before pressure hits.

My action steps
Action step 1: Build a simple campaign plan (goal, audience, creative, budget, timeline)

Use this structure.

Goal
Be specific.
Examples:

- 100 new followers in the city
- 30 new inquiries in 2 weeks
- 20 orders for a new product drop
- 10 repeat buyers this month

Audience
Who exactly are you targeting?
Location, interests, age range, language.

Creative
What content will you use?

- one boosted reel
- one proof carousel
- stories daily
- one live Q and A
- one offer post

Budget
How much can you spend without pain?
Small budgets are fine.
Clarity matters more than size.

Timeline
Set dates:

- start date
- end date
- review date

Now write your campaign plan:

Campaign name:
Goal:
Audience:
Creative:
Budget:
Timeline:
Tracking method:
Expected outcome:

Action step 2: Create a "press ready" brand pack

Your brand pack is a small folder you can send quickly.

Include:

Short bio (50 to 80 words)
Who you are, what you do, who you serve.

Short brand story (150 to 250 words)
Origin, mission, values, what makes you different.

Product or service photos
High quality images.
Clean background if possible.
Different angles.
Lifestyle usage if possible.

Logo and brand assets
Logo files, colors, fonts.

Contact details
Email, phone/WhatsApp, website link, location.

One-page offer summary
What you sell, price range, ordering steps.

Create this as one folder in your storage system:
PRESS READY PACK

Then you are ready for opportunities.

Action step 3: Write my growth rules

This is your identity protection contract.

Growth brings temptation:

- to exaggerate
- to copy
- to cut corners
- to accept shady partnerships
- to chase attention at any cost

Your growth rules protect you.

Write them now.

Examples:

- I will not lie to get attention.
- I will not fake testimonials.
- I will not partner with brands that contradict my values.
- I will not sacrifice quality to fulfill more orders.
- I will not respond with anger in public.
- I will not chase trends that make me look fake.
- I will not compromise cultural respect for jokes or clicks.

Now create your own list.

Put it where you can see it.

Because when pressure rises, memory becomes weak.

Rules keep you steady.

Closing lesson for this chapter

Beyond the basics is not about becoming loud.

It is about becoming ready.

Creator partnerships should feel like trust, not performance.
Paid promotion should amplify what already works, not rescue what is weak.
Attention must be turned into a real business system with clear offers and strong support.
Cultural sensitivity protects your brand when you go global.
Opportunities reward preparation.

When you grow with maturity, your brand does not just get bigger.

It becomes stronger.

Appendices and tools (copy-and-use)

These appendices are designed to be practical. You can copy them into a notebook, a note app, or a document, and start using them immediately.

They are not theory.

They are tools.

Use them to build consistency, protect your energy, and turn social media into a predictable system that creates awareness, trust, and business outcomes.

Appendix A: 30-day digital visibility plan

This plan assumes you have one primary platform and one support platform.

Primary platform examples:
Instagram, TikTok, Facebook, LinkedIn, YouTube Shorts

Support platform examples:
Facebook group, WhatsApp, email list, YouTube long-form, a blog

If you only have one platform, that is fine. Use the plan anyway.

The goal of the 30 days

- Build consistent visibility without burnout
- Create trust through repetition
- Generate a steady stream of replies and inquiries
- Learn what content your audience responds to most

Your setup (do this on Day 1)

Primary platform:
Support platform:

Your offer (what you sell or want to lead toward):
Your main audience (one sentence):
Your 30-day outcome goal (one clear goal):

Examples:

- 30 inquiries
- 10 sales
- 100 new followers in my city
- 20 repeat buyers
- 5 collaboration leads

Your weekly rhythm

Each week you will do the same cycle:

Create
Schedule
Engage
Review

Daily minimums (every day, 15 to 30 minutes)

- Post 3 to 7 story frames (or 1 short update if stories are not your platform)
- Reply to comments and DMs in two windows
- Leave 5 meaningful comments on other pages in your niche

Weekly posting plan (choose one)

Option 1: 3 posts per week

- 1 teach
- 1 show/proof
- 1 sell/invite

Option 2: 5 posts per week

- 2 teach

- 2 show/proof
- 1 sell/invite

Week 1: Build foundations and clarity

Focus: profile clarity + trust signals

Tasks:

- Clean bio and profile
- Create 3 pinned posts: Start here, Proof, Offer
- Create highlights: Start here, Proof, How to order, FAQs

Content:

- Teach post: "What I help with and why it matters"
- Show post: behind the scenes or process proof
- Invite post: question or poll to learn audience language
- Sell post: simple offer with clear next step

Weekly review questions:

- What did people reply to most?
- What questions kept showing up?
- Which post earned saves or shares?

Week 2: Build community and conversation

Focus: participation loops

Tasks:

- Create a simple community hashtag
- Launch a weekly ritual (prompt, challenge, spotlight)

Content:

- Teach post: practical checklist or lesson

- Show post: proof, delivery, process, testimonial
- Invite post: "choose one" or "tell me your situation"
- Sell post: offer tied to the week's teaching
- Stories: polls, Q and A, repost follower replies

Weekly review questions:

- Did comments increase?
- Did story replies increase?
- Which prompt created the most participation?

Week 3: Build offers and lead flow

Focus: turn attention into action

Tasks:

- Create a DM keyword system for tracking (example: message me "PLAN")
- Write ordering steps and save reply templates
- Create a link hub or one clear link

Content:

- Teach post: "how to choose the right option" or "mistakes to avoid"
- Show post: customer story and result
- Invite post: ask what people want next
- Sell post: a clear offer with a deadline or limited slots (only if real)

Weekly review questions:

- How many DMs with buying intent did you get?
- How many link clicks happened?
- Which content led to inquiries?

Week 4: Build advocacy and repeat visibility

Focus: turn buyers and followers into promoters

Tasks:

- Run a mini UGC campaign (prompt + hashtag + spotlight)
- Feature customers or community members
- Do one collaboration or joint live (if possible)

Content:

- Teach post: strongest lesson of the month, refined
- Show post: montage of proof and testimonials
- Invite post: UGC prompt
- Sell post: offer + proof + next step
- Stories: highlight participants, shoutouts, thank you messages

Weekly review questions:

- Who advocated publicly?
- Which proof content built trust fastest?
- What will you repeat next month?

Appendix B: Weekly content calendar template (copy and fill)

Week of:
Primary goal:

Pillar 1:
Pillar 2:
Pillar 3:

Monday
Post type:
Topic:

Format:
CTA:

Tuesday
Stories focus:
Engagement focus:

Wednesday
Post type:
Topic:
Format:
CTA:

Thursday
Stories focus:
Engagement focus:

Friday
Post type:
Topic:
Format:
CTA:

Saturday
Optional post or series:
Stories focus:

Sunday
Review + planning:
What worked:
What didn't:
Next test:

Appendix C: Content pillar planner and idea bank
Pillar planner (copy)

Pillar name:
Audience need it serves:

What I will teach/show:
Proof I can share:
Offers tied to this pillar:

Repeat for three pillars.

Idea bank (top 30 prompts)

Teach prompts

- "3 mistakes people make with _____"
- "How to do _____ in 5 steps"
- "What I wish I knew before _____"
- "If you only do one thing this week, do this: _____"
- "The simplest way to improve _____"

Show prompts

- "Behind the scenes: how I do _____"
- "Before and after: _____"
- "A day in my work: _____"
- "What I check before I deliver _____"
- "The tools I use for _____"

Invite prompts

- "Which one are you: A or B?"
- "What is your biggest challenge with _____?"
- "Tell me your goal for this week"
- "If I made a guide on _____, would you want it?"
- "Vote: what should I cover next?"

Sell prompts

- "Here's what's available this week"
- "This is for people who need _____"
- "If you want help with _____, here's the next step"
- "Limited slots for _____ (only if real)"
- "Customer spotlight + how to order"

Appendix D: Caption formulas and call-to-action bank

Caption formulas

Formula 1: Hook, teach, proof, invite
Hook:
Lesson:
Proof:
Invite:

Formula 2: Micro-story (moment, meaning, lesson)
Moment:
Meaning:
Lesson:
Invite:

Formula 3: Problem, truth, steps, next step
Problem:
Truth:
Steps:
Next step:

Formula 4: Myth, reality, action
Myth:
Reality:
Action:

Formula 5: FAQ style
Question:
Answer:
Proof:
Next step:

Call-to-action bank

Engagement CTAs

- "Save this for later"

- "Share this with a friend"
- "Comment with your situation"
- "Vote: A or B"
- "What would you add?"

Lead CTAs

- "Message me 'PLAN' and I'll send the details"
- "Click the link in my bio"
- "Reply to this story with 'YES'"
- "Send your location and I'll confirm pricing"

Sales CTAs

- "To order, message me with your size and location"
- "Slots open for this week. Want one?"
- "Would you like me to reserve this for you today?"

Advocacy CTAs

- "Tag me when you post yours"
- "Use our hashtag so I can repost you"
- "If you loved this, tell a friend who needs it"

Appendix E: Hashtag worksheet (including movement hashtag setup)
Hashtag categories

Brand hashtag (your name or brand)
Example format: #BrandName

Community hashtag (belonging)
Example format: #BrandCircle

Movement hashtag (meaning and identity)
Example format: #StitchesOfStrength

Content hashtags (topic)
Example: #SocialMediaTips #SmallBusinessMarketing

Local hashtags (location)
Example: #NairobiBusiness #JubaEntrepreneurs

Hashtag worksheet (copy)

Brand hashtag:
Community hashtag:
Movement hashtag:

Movement meaning (one sentence):
Who is it for:
What does it stand for:
What kind of posts should use it:
How I will feature users of the hashtag:

Movement hashtag setup steps

- choose a unique phrase that is easy to remember
- define the meaning in one sentence
- use it consistently in your series content
- feature people who use it
- tie it to a monthly campaign

Appendix F: Community rules and moderation scripts
Community rules (copy and edit)

- Respect people. No insults.
- No hate speech or tribal attacks.
- No spam or self-promotion without permission.
- Disagree with ideas, not with dignity.
- If you have a complaint, share it respectfully so we can fix it.

Moderation scripts

Script 1: gentle warning
"Please keep this space respectful. If you have a real concern, share it without insults."

Script 2: boundary statement
"We remove disrespectful comments to protect the community. You are welcome to return with a respectful tone."

Script 3: redirect to DM
"I hear your concern. Please message me so we can handle this privately and properly."

Script 4: final action statement
"This comment violates our community rules, so it has been removed."

Appendix G: Customer message templates (DM replies, order confirmation, follow-up)

Pricing reply
"Thanks for asking. The price is _____. Which option do you want, and what is your location?"

Availability reply
"Yes, it is available. Do you want pickup or delivery?"

Delivery reply
"Yes, I deliver. Please send your location and preferred delivery time."

Order confirmation
"Confirmed. Item: _____. Price: _____. Delivery: _____. Time: _____. Payment method: _____. I will update you once it is on the way."

Follow-up after delivery
"Thank you again for trusting my work. Did everything arrive well? If you want, share a photo and tag me so I can repost."

Complaint handling
"Thank you for telling me. I'm sorry about this. Please share your order details and what went wrong so I can fix it quickly."

Referral request
"If you know someone who would benefit from this, feel free to share my page or tag me. I'll take care of them the same way."

Appendix H: Simple analytics sheet and monthly review template

Weekly scorecard (copy)

Week of:
Primary goal:

Reach:
Saves:
Shares:
Buying-intent DMs:
Sales or leads:

Notes:
What worked:
What didn't:
One change next week:

Monthly review template (copy)

Month:
Primary goal:

Wins:
Losses:
Lessons:

Next tests (two only):
What I will repeat:
What I will stop:

Appendix I: Low-data creation tips for limited internet environments

- Write captions offline in a notes app.
- Record videos in batches, then upload during strong Wi-Fi windows.
- Use simple edits. Clean cuts beat heavy effects.
- Compress videos before upload if needed.
- Turn one idea into multiple formats to reduce creation load.
- Use stories as light touch when you can't upload heavy content.
- Keep your templates saved: caption formulas, story slides, replies.
- Save drafts inside the app when possible, then publish later.
- Use one primary platform to avoid spreading thin.

Appendix J: Glossary of key social media marketing terms

Advocacy
Repeated public support from followers or customers.

Algorithm
The system platforms use to decide what content to show to whom.

Attribution
How you assign credit for a sale or lead.

Call to action (CTA)
A direct request for the viewer to take a next step.

Carousel
A multi-slide post used for teaching, proof, or storytelling.

Content pillar
A core category of themes you post about repeatedly.

Conversion
When a viewer takes a business action, like buying or signing up.

Engagement
Actions people take: likes, comments, saves, shares, replies.

Funnel
The journey from awareness to trust to purchase.

Lead
A person who shows interest and may buy.

Reach
How many unique accounts see your content.

Repurposing
Turning one idea into multiple pieces of content.

UGC (user-generated content)
Content made by customers or followers featuring your brand.

Watch time
How long people watch your video, a strong signal for platforms.

BACK MATTER

Final Note to the Reader

Thank you for finishing this book.

That matters more than most people realize.

In a world of endless scrolling, finishing anything is a sign of discipline. It shows that you are not only consuming information. You are building a life and a business with intention.

I wrote this book for one reason: to help you stop treating social media like a lottery and start treating it like a system.

A system you can run even when your internet is unstable.
A system you can run even when your confidence is low.
A system you can run even when your audience is small.

Because social media is not magic.

It is visibility plus trust plus follow-through.

When you show up consistently, people notice.
When you show up with integrity, people believe.
When you show up with a clear offer and solid support, people buy.
When you treat buyers like humans, not numbers, they return.
When you build community, people advocate for you.
When you measure honestly, you improve without panic.
When you adapt wisely, you grow without losing your identity.

If you take nothing else from this book, take this:

You do not need to become loud to be seen.
You need to become clear.

Clarity is kindness.
Clarity is confidence.
Clarity is what helps the right people find you and trust you.

Now the real work begins.

Not in theory.

In practice.

Start with the 30-day visibility plan.
Choose one platform.
Choose one goal.
Run the weekly workflow.
Track your five numbers.
Improve one thing at a time.

And keep your dignity.

Your brand is your name in public.
Protect it.
Grow it.
Let it be known for honesty and quality.

If you ever feel discouraged, remember this:

The internet rewards consistency more than perfection.

Show up.
Serve well.
Learn fast.
Stay true.

I am cheering for you.

Leave a Review (three prompts)

If this book helped you, please consider leaving a review. Reviews help other readers find the book and decide whether it is worth their time.

Here are three simple prompts you can use:

What was the biggest lesson you learned from this book, and why did it matter to you?

Which tool or appendix did you actually use or plan to use first, and what result are you hoping for?

Who would you recommend this book to, and what kind of business or goal do you think it fits best?

Thank you for taking a minute to do that. It truly helps.

Order and bulk copies

If you would like to order multiple copies for your team, your organization, a training program, a school, a church group, or a business community, bulk orders are available.

Bulk copies are useful for:

- entrepreneurship and small business training
- community business groups and cultural organizations
- social media and marketing workshops
- youth empowerment programs
- staff development for customer-facing teams

For bulk orders, training use, or special requests, contact:

Email: maluthabiel@gmail.com
Phone/WhatsApp: +211 927 145 394
Website: www.johnshalom.com

ABOUT THE AUTHOR

John Monyjok Maluth is a writer, teacher, and coach focused on building meaningful lives through clarity, integrity, and practical action. He writes for entrepreneurs, creators, and everyday people who want to grow without losing themselves.

John's work is shaped by lived experience across South Sudan, East Africa, and beyond. He has built digital projects, taught students and leaders, and helped organizations and individuals communicate with purpose. He believes that true success is not only about numbers, but about becoming the kind of person who can carry growth with maturity.

His guiding principle is simple:

Meaning comes from identity and intentional action.

When you know who you are and you do the work with discipline, your life and your business become stronger.

Website: www.johnshalom.com
Email: maluthabiel@gmail.com
Phone/WhatsApp: +211 927 145 394

www.ingramcontent.com/pod-product-compliance
Lightning Source LLC
Chambersburg PA
CBHW031618210526
45464CB00004B/1640